All About
Moths and Butterflies

All About Moths and Butterflies

By Robert S. Lemmon

Illustrated by Fritz Kredel

RANDOM HOUSE
NEW YORK

THIRD PRINTING

© COPYRIGHT, 1956, BY ROBERT S. LEMMON

All rights reserved under International and Pan-American copyright Conventions. Published in New York by Random House, Inc., and simultaneously in Toronto, Canada, by Random House of Canada, Limited.

LIBRARY OF CONGRESS CATALOG CARD NUMBER: 56-5467

MANUFACTURED IN THE UNITED STATES OF AMERICA

All About
Moths and Butterflies

Contents

BUTTERFLY DAYS AND WAYS

HOW TO STUDY MOTHS AND BUTTERFLIES

The Tribe
With Scaly Wings

Family Traits

Would you like to know more about moths and butterflies? I mean strange facts such as how they grow and live, what their youngsters are like, why their colors are so amazing, and the reasons for their countless sizes and shapes? There are so many of them and there is so much to know about them, that it's hard to know where to start.

To begin with, you can think of all these insects as being one huge family of more or less related cousins.

Scientists believe that their oldest ancestors appeared on earth at least fifty million years ago. They know this because parts of them have been found in rocks as old as that. By now many thousands of different kinds have developed and more are being discovered every year all over the world. Right here in the United States and Canada there are at least three times as many moth species as there are butterflies. Yet it is the butterflies that you usually see, because most moths stay hidden all day.

Insect authorities call this great tribe the Order Lepidoptera. The name Lepidoptera comes from two Greek words meaning "scale" and "wing." It fits moths and butterflies perfectly, for the wings of almost all of them are covered with sheets of tiny scales that overlap each other like shingles on a roof. The end of each one is attached to the wing's "skin" as if it were a feather.

These scales are different from those on a fish. Instead of being fairly large and rough, they are soft and so small that they rub off on your fingers like dust when you touch them. There are scales on the insects' bodies and legs, too. But these are longer and more like hairs.

All Lepidoptera scales are tremendously interesting to

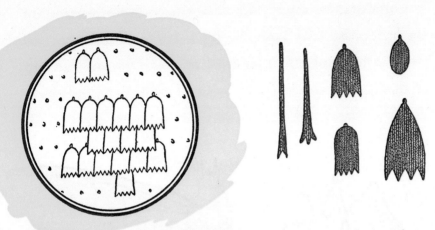

The wing scales of a moth as seen through a magnifying glass.

look at through a strong magnifying glass. And if you should see them through a microscope, they would seem still more marvelous.

The wing scales of moths as well as butterflies help their owners in two important ways. For one thing, they make the wings stronger. And in the second place, they provide the colors which make the wings of most species so wonderfully beautiful. If all the scales were taken off, there just wouldn't be any colors. And you could see right through the wings almost as easily as if they were made of cellophane.

There are lots of other ways, too, in which all the Lepidoptera are alike.

All About Moths and Butterflies

For instance, every one of them has four wings and six legs. Also, the body is divided into three principal parts: the head; the middle body or *thorax*; and the stomach and digesting part, which is called the *abdomen*. A quick look will explain how they work.

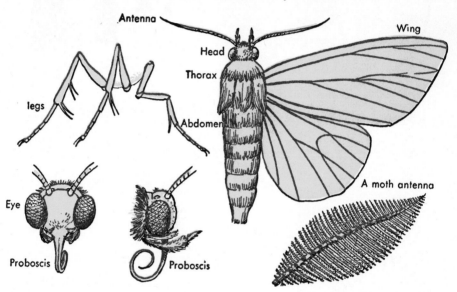

Most of the space in the head is taken up by two big eyes, each with many very small lenses in it. These eyes cannot move as ours do. But their rounded shape makes the thousands of lenses in them aim in all kinds of directions. The result is that the insect can see ahead, upward, sideways, down and backwards all at the same time.

Another very important part of the head is the hollow

tongue or feeding tube, called the *proboscis*. It is completely different from what we all think of as a tongue. It is really made up of two half-tubes stuck together so that they form a single larger one. The insect uses it to suck in nectar, which is the sweet, nourishing liquid hidden far down in the center of many flowers.

The sucking action of this feeding tube is produced by a sort of bulb at its inside end. This works somewhat like the rubber bulb on an eye dropper. But there is this big difference: when the insect's muscles squeeze the tongue bulb, the liquid goes down its throat. But when you squeeze a full eye dropper, the medicine squirts out at the other end.

When a moth or butterfly is not using its proboscis, it keeps it rolled up under its mouth as if it were a coiled watch spring. In one kind of hawk moth it is ten inches long when straightened out. That is about six times as long as the moth's entire body.

Another astonishing part of the head is the pair of many-jointed "feelers," or *antennae*, which stick out between the eyes. These two little gadgets are the insect's nose, and they can smell things ever so much better than our noses can. Some scientists believe that they serve as ears, too. And it is possible that they can pick up other information which is quite different from anything that we are able to get through our senses of sight, hearing, taste and touch.

Just behind the head you come to the *thorax*. This is the part of the body from which the wings and all of the legs grow. It has three connected sections. Each of these carries a pair of legs, one on each side. The middle section is the anchor for the front wings, also. And the rear wings are attached to the last section.

Moth and butterfly legs are built in five parts. The two nearest the body form what is called a "universal" joint. This can move in all directions, like your own hip joint. Then comes a long, thicker section which takes the place of your thigh. Next to this is the *tibia*, where you have a shinbone. And finally there is the *tarsus*, which connects the tibia with a short jointed part that is a sort of foot. Each pair of legs is a little different from the others. But on all of them there are a few tiny spurs that help the insect to cling to a flower or some other perch.

The four wings of moths and butterflies are even more peculiar. Each one has a framework of hard, springy, double tubes called *veins*. The inner tube of each vein is filled with air. And the outer one carries green or yellow blood which circulates in more or less the same way that your red blood does through your arteries and veins.

You can see this strange network if you carefully rub off the scales from both sides of a wing. And then you will discover, also, the very thin layers of "skin," one on each side, which cover and connect all the veins.

It is this airtight skin, of course, that permits all insects of the Order Lepidoptera to fly. You see, it supports them by pressing against the air when they flap their wings or glide between wing beats. When a bird flies, it gets the same sort of results by pushing on the air with its wing feathers.

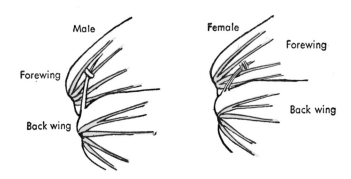

This drawing shows how forewing and back wing hook together.

Another odd fact is that the rear edges of the front wings, and the front edges of the back ones, are either curved or fitted with rows of fine bristles. These curves or bristles hook together when the insect flies. In this way the front and back wings can make a single unbroken surface on each side of the body.

What Happens Inside?

All these things we have been talking about are the most important *outside* parts of a moth or butterfly. Now let's see what goes on *inside* its body.

First, these insects have no hearts, as we understand the meaning of that word. Instead, the blood is pushed along through thin tubes that shiver rapidly from one end to the other. Each shiver takes the place of one of your heart beats. And, because all the shivers move in the same direction, they keep the blood moving through the whole system of veins and arteries.

Another network of tubes does the job of regular lungs. The air goes in and out through little holes, called *spiracles*, on the sides of the body. Moths, as well as butterflies, breathe a great deal faster than we do. This is partly because their breathing system is so small.

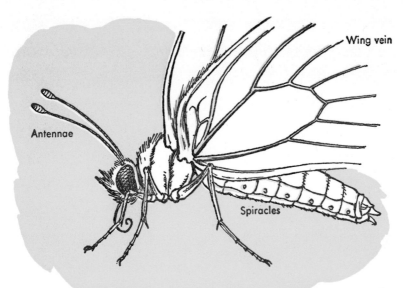

Air goes in and out through little holes called spiracles.

Here is another surprise: none of the Lepidoptera has a regular brain. There are plenty of nerves, though. Most of the main ones run lengthwise along the lower side of the body, instead of up and down the back as ours do. There are many little bunches or knots of nerves in various parts of the body. You might call these control towers, for they help to manage the parts of the insect which are nearest to them.

The largest of these little nerve bunches are in the head, where the *optic nerves* connect with the eyes. Moths and butterflies cannot see as well as we do. Beyond a couple of yards they probably cannot do much more than tell light from dark. But they must have very sharp sight in all directions at close range. This helps them to spot their enemies and also see exactly what they are doing when they feed.

Most of these delicate creatures have a great many more separate muscles than we do—sometimes thousands more. The largest ones are in the thorax, where their main purpose is to operate the wings and legs. The rest are scattered all through the body, head, wings and legs. Most of them are so small that you cannot see them at all without a good microscope.

When it comes to swallowing and digesting their food, these insects are not so different from ourselves as you might expect. As you know, they live chiefly on the nectar which they suck out of flowers. It is pulled in through the proboscis, as you might drink a soda through a couple of straws. Then it goes into the throat and finally gets to the real stomach. That is where the job of digesting the nectar is done.

Are you wondering what kinds of bones moths and butterflies have? The answer is short and simple: they don't have any bones at all—anywhere! There would not be room for a bony framework inside such fragile little creatures. So, instead of bones, they are covered with a thin suit of armor that protects their softness and holds everything in place. You might call it a sort of outside skeleton.

This remarkable covering is just outside the true skin. It is made of *chitin*, which you pronounce as if it were spelled *ki-tin*. (It almost rhymes with *brighten*.) And there are so many close fitting, perfect joints in it that the insect can turn and twist and wriggle in practically any direction.

Chitin is formed from a liquid produced inside the insect's body. This liquid hardens until it is a good deal like a very, very thin toenail. The older it gets the stronger it becomes. Although it does not stretch and weighs next to nothing, it never turns brittle the way an old bone does. It makes a first-rate anchorage for all the tiny muscles which are attached to the inside.

The whole arrangement seems just right for creatures that are nearly as light as feathers and sometimes fly as fast as twenty miles an hour!

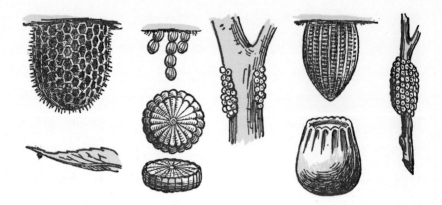

Moth and butterfly eggs are of many kinds, shapes and sizes.

Growing Up

Every moth and butterfly has to go through three stages before it can fly. The first of these is the egg. Next comes the caterpillar or *larva*. And the third one is the chrysalis or *pupa*. This is an astonishing stage during which the larva remains almost motionless while it slowly changes its form completely!

Moths and butterflies begin life inside very small eggs laid by the full-grown female. When the time comes to lay them, she hunts for some particular kind of plant whose leaves the youngsters will like to eat when they hatch. The best sort may be an oak tree, a spicebush, a maple, a milkweed, a grapevine or something else. Almost every moth and butterfly species has its favorites. Usually it can recognize them by the way the leaves smell.

When she finds the right plant, the mother insect begins to lay her eggs. Usually she sticks them on the undersides of the leaves where they will be protected from rain and hot sun. When she has finished, she may have laid from a few to several hundred, depending on her species. Some kinds place their eggs singly, perhaps only one on each leaf. Others lay them in small clusters, in rings or in one large mass.

Each egg may be no larger than a pinhead, but it is wonderfully perfect. It may be blue, green, brown, red, yellow or white, depending on what species laid it. It may have darker markings, too. Some kinds are barrel-shaped. Others are angular, half-round, conical or as round as tiny balls. Very often they have ridges on them which form beautiful patterns. All the eggs of any particular species of moth or butterfly look exactly alike.

Inside the egg is the germ of the future caterpillar. There is also enough liquid food to make it grow until it is big enough to hatch. Some kinds will not hatch for months. But a great many species of baby caterpillars will be ready to chew their way through their prisons and crawl out into the open air a few days or a few weeks after the eggs were laid.

The first thing the little fellows do when they get out is to start crawling and eating. They almost never stop chewing and swallowing bits of their favorite leaves.

They gobble so much and grow so fast that you can hardly believe it. For instance, a larva of our beautiful polyphemus moth will eat eighty-six thousand times its own hatching weight in the first forty-eight hours. When it comes out of the egg, it is only a small fraction of an inch long. But after seven weeks it is fully grown, measures three inches from end to end, and is as thick as your finger.

Caterpillar eyes are very small. Probably they cannot see too well. But their owner has other ways of finding its way around. One of these is by using a pair of little antennae. And another is the help it gets from two sets of tiny objects called *palpi*. The palpi are organs of touch. They are located on the lips and apparently are very useful in guiding the weak-eyed caterpillar.

Of course there are also *mandibles*, or jaws, with which to chew. And many species have a tiny horny device called a *spinneret*. This is on the upper lip, too. There is a very fine hole in it through which a silk-making fluid inside the larva's head can be squeezed out. As soon as this fluid reaches the open air, it hardens into an astonishingly thin but strong silk thread.

The bodies of most moth and butterfly caterpillars are divided into thirteen sections or *segments*. There are joints between these so that the whole body can bend in any direction. The whole arrangement is somewhat like thirteen very small hoops lined up close to each other and covered with very thin rubber or elastic cloth.

A caterpillar's body segments permit it to twist and turn.

When you think of it this way, you can understand how the caterpillar can stretch out, squinch itself together, or bend into a circle without breaking anything.

Most caterpillar species have seven or eight pairs of legs spread along the body from head to tail. Those near the front are short, thin and curved. All the rest are fat, straight and stubby. The whole crowd makes quite a procession as their owner creeps along a leaf or twig by hanging on with some pairs while it reaches forward with others.

Above the legs, and on each side of the body, there is a row of little breathing holes. The full-grown winged insect will have the same sort of spiracles, as you know.

All moth and butterfly larvae have thin and often loose-fitting skins. Their owners grow so fast, though, that the ones they have been wearing soon become too small for them. Then an odd thing happens. The caterpillar fastens itself to a twig or leaf with a bit of home-made silk from its spinneret and stays quiet for a while. Finally the old skin splits from end to end. Then the caterpillar crawls out in a brand new but larger suit.

This change to larger-size clothes is called a *molt*. It

may be repeated four or five times before the caterpillar is full-grown. Except for its greater size, each new skin is almost always like the one it replaces. Most kinds are green or brownish, like the surroundings in which the caterpillar lives. Some show several bright colors. Many species have perfectly smooth skins, but hundreds of others are dotted with bumps, spines, hairs or "horns" to protect them. But you had better not touch a hairy or spiny one, for its protections may be poisonous to your skin.

Nearly all these amazing caterpillars of the Order Lepidoptera lead lonely lives. You seldom see even two of the same species close to each other. But a few kinds, such as the tent caterpillar, live in crowds or colonies. Often these family groups spin large and complicated waterproof webs into which they crawl at night or in stormy weather. "Tents" like these help protect them from their enemies, too.

Good-bye to Caterpillar Days

A caterpillar's life may last from a few weeks to more than a year. This depends on what species it is. But always, when the creature is fully grown, it undergoes an

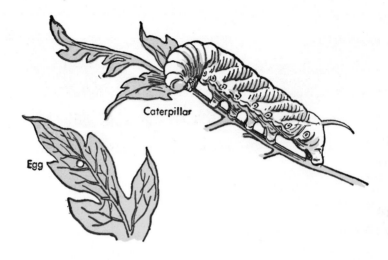

Caterpillar

Egg

Every moth and butterfly goes through three stages before it can fly. The first is the egg which develops into a caterpillar.

astonishing change. The time has now come for the crawling "worm" to quit being a caterpillar and become what is called a *pupa*. This *pupal* stage is perhaps the most unbelievable one in the whole life history of any moth or butterfly.

It happens this way:

First, the larva stops eating and begins to look for a good place where it can turn into a pupa. This search may take it as far as a hundred feet or more. Many of the moth caterpillars burrow into the ground and make their pupal change there. Others creep under loose tree bark, dead leaves, flat stones or brush piles. Some choose

Hawk moth

Pupa

The caterpillar or larva turns into a chrysalis or pupa. Much later the wormlike creature turns into a moth or butterfly.

sheltered boards inside a shed or behind the shutters of a house. And some others *pupate* inside rolled-up leaves or on the stem of a plant.

In almost every case a moth caterpillar spins at least some silk around itself before it starts to change. Where a lot of silk is used, the hiding place is called a *cocoon*. Cocoons are made only by moth caterpillars. Butterfly species have a different way of pupating.

Inside the darkness of this little cell, strange events take place during the fall and winter. There is no room for the moth larva to turn around. But somehow it manages to wriggle out of its old and largest skin. Then the whole crawling creature begins to turn into a winged moth. A coat of wonderful shiny chitin slowly grows over it.

Inside this covering, four wings begin to form, and so do six legs much longer and thinner than the old ones. New and different eyes and antennae develop. The mouth changes, and that wonderful sucking proboscis starts to grow. Practically everything that was like a caterpillar disappears. And for weeks and months the plain brown pupa lies motionless while it grows into an entirely new and very beautiful insect!

Spring is the time when most moth species leave their pupal homes. Those pupas, or *pupae*, which have been hidden underground wriggle their way to the surface. There the chitin coverings open, and the new but badly crumpled moths struggle out. Other kinds which pupated in above-ground cocoons have a different way of emerging. First they shed their pupal coats inside the cocoons. Then they dissolve the silken walls at one end of their cells with a special liquid that comes from their mouths. After this they struggle and struggle until finally they escape.

No moths are able to fly when they first get out into the open air. Their wings are small and badly crumpled.

Their bodies are so long and flabby that they look almost like worms. Any enemy could easily catch them. Something must be done—and fast!

So each one starts crawling around like mad. It must get to a twig or some other object where it can cling with its feet and let its wings and body hang straight down. When it finds such a place, it begins slowly to fan its crumpled wings. This starts the blood circulating and brings nourishment and strength to them.

Soon the wings commence to straighten out. As they lose their wrinkles, they become larger and stronger. The body gets shorter, too, because the strengthening liquids in it have been spread by the blood circulation to all other parts that need them.

At last the wings and the rest of the new insect are full-sized and ready to go. Then the softly beautiful young moth flits away as easily as if it had been flying for weeks or even months.

The Quick-Change Artist

The egg and larva stages of a butterfly are much like those of a moth. But when the larva gets ready to become a pupa, it acts quite differently.

Very few kinds of butterfly caterpillars make what

you could call real cocoons. Instead, they begin by building a little "button" of silk with their spinnerets. This button is firmly fastened to the underside of a twig, plant stem or some other projecting object. Some species also spin a silk safety belt around themselves and fasten its ends to the twig.

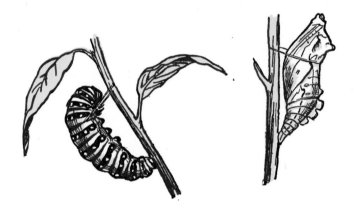

This caterpillar has made a silk safety belt which fastens it to the stem of a plant.

Next, the caterpillar takes hold of the silk button with the pair of legs nearest its tail. It also gets a second hold on the button with a strange little tail hook called a *cremaster*. This hook is covered with skin, just as the legs are. Finally, the caterpillar lets go with all its other legs so that it hangs head downward.

In this upside-down position, it sheds its old skin. It does this by twisting and wriggling so that the skin is worked backward and upward all the way from the head to the tail end.

The caterpillar is now up against a real problem. It must get its last pair of hind legs, and also the cremaster, out of the old skin. But the grip of that skin on the silk button is all that keeps the larva from falling to the ground and spoiling everything.

At this point an unbelievable thing happens. The caterpillar catches some of the loose, shed skin tightly between the edges of its rear sections or "hoops." This will keep it from falling while those last legs and the cremaster are getting out of the old skin which still covers them.

The final trick is the best one of all. The moment the cremaster hook slips out of its skin, it reaches for that silk button and gets a fresh grip. This is such a strong hold that the pupa can hang there safely until the time comes for the adult butterfly to crawl out of it.

Everything is now ready for the castoff skin of the butterfly larva to be replaced by a hard cover of chitin. As you know, moth species make a similar replacement.

All About Moths and Butterflies

Also, both moth and butterfly larvae, inside these tough pupal coverings, change into adults in the same sort of way. An adult butterfly, however, may emerge in a few weeks. Many other species, and practically all of the moths, stay in the pupal stage all winter and come out in the spring.

Some butterfly pupae, or *chrysalises*, are much prettier than those of moths. There are plain green ones, and others are green spotted with gold. Some are various shades of brown and yellow. And a great many have bumps and points and ridges which make them strangely beautiful.

Is It a Moth or a Butterfly?

Moths and butterflies are so much alike in many ways that you are probably wondering how to tell them apart. Just what are the important differences which you can see?

Well, for one thing, most moths do their flying late in the evening, at night, or very early in the morning. During the day they rest and sleep among bushes or in other safe hiding places. You seldom see one on the wing in broad daylight.

Butterflies do just the opposite. They are day fliers and night sleepers. It is true that some kinds live in the deep woods where everything is fairly dark even at mid-day. But most species like plenty of sunlight when they go looking for food.

The slender, many-jointed antennae projecting from the head are another good way of telling one group from another. Moth antennae are generally thicker at the base than out toward the end. In a few cases they are smooth from one end to the other. But usually they have little hairlike or comblike fringes along one or both sides. These fringes may be so short that you can hardly see them without a magnifying glass. In many other species they are long enough to make each antenna look like a slender little feather. And some kinds are so heavily

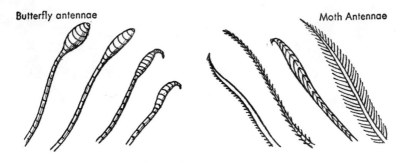

Butterfly antennae

Moth Antennae

With a magnifying glass you can see the difference between the antennae of butterflies and those of moths.

fringed that they remind you of broad, wonderfully beautiful plumes.

The antennae of butterflies are quite different. They have no fringes at all. They are said to be "clubbed" because their thickest part is at the tip or close to it. Quite often the tip itself is curved somewhat like a fish-hook. All these butterfly antennae are very slender where they join the insect's head.

The shape of the body is another way of telling a moth from a butterfly. In moths, the body is quite thick in proportion to its length. It may be rather wedge-shaped, too, with the broadest part near the front. And the hair scales on it are so long and thick that they often

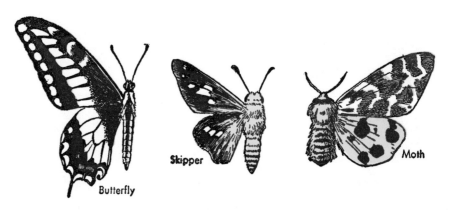

Butterfly   Skipper   Moth

The body of a moth is broader than that of a butterfly.

look like real fur.

True butterfly bodies are generally slender and the hair scales are much shorter. But this is not always the case. In one very large group of butterflies, known as skippers, the bodies are so stout that you might think they belonged to moths. This is one of the reasons why scientists believe that moths and butterflies are related to each other. They think that maybe the skippers are a sort of connecting link between these two great branches of the Order Lepidoptera.

There is another way in which moths and butterflies are different from each other. In general, moth colors are softer and less showy than those of butterflies. This

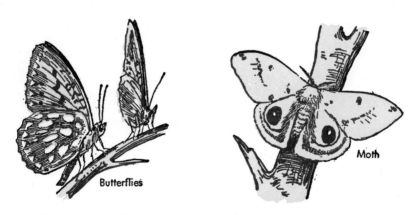

Butterflies

Moth

A butterfly holds its wings upright; the moth spreads his.

is especially true in the case of those small moth species which most of us call "millers." Perhaps this has something to do with the fact that moths are active only when there is little if any real daylight. Sometimes the stronger, brighter colors of so many day-flying butterflies really make it harder for their enemies to catch them. You see, mixed-up, bright colors often make first-class camouflage.

Perhaps the best way of deciding whether an insect is a moth or a butterfly is to watch what it does with its wings while perching or moving about slowly on its legs. At such times a butterfly generally holds its wings upright and close together over its back. Occasionally they will spread a little, and then close again. But a moth's wings seldom take such a position. They are more likely to be held almost straight out from the insect's sides and pointing a little backward. These differences do not fit all moth and butterfly species. But they are well worth watching for.

Moths, the Fly-by-Nights

Very Special Species

To understand the way moths and butterflies are built and the stages they pass through, it is important to take a closer look at some of the most interesting kinds of these featherweight insects.

One of the loveliest is the yellow and pale brown royal walnut moth. Royal, the first half of its odd name, comes from its size and great beauty. And the second half was chosen because, as a caterpillar, it is particularly fond of eating the leaves of walnut, butternut and hickory trees.

Royal walnut moth

Hickory horned-devil

The beautiful royal walnut moth comes from this ugly larva.

You might think that such a handsome moth must be good-looking even while it is still a caterpillar. But it is exactly the opposite of that. In fact, the hickory horned-devil, as the royal walnut's larva is called, looks like something you'd meet in an awful nightmare.

Up near its head there are six rough, curved, orange and black "horns." Sharp spines are scattered all over its green, white and black body. It has three pairs of orange legs and four pairs of black and yellow ones. When fully grown it may be six or seven inches long. And when it is frightened, it raises its front end into the air like some kind of dragon!

In some parts of our country this fearsome caterpillar and its beautiful parents are quite rare. In New Jersey, where I grew up, I remember seeing only two of the adult moths. Both of them were fluttering late at night around an arc light at a street corner in a country village.

Several years earlier I had found my first hickory horned-devil in the edge of the woods behind our house. I was examining some badly chewed leaves on the lowest branch of a hickory tree. And suddenly, there was the big

Luna moth

The wings of the luna moth often spread five inches across.

caterpillar only a couple of feet from my face. I must have jumped a yard. But the hickory horned-devil did not seem to be scared at all.

Another beauty among our large moths is the luna. This one is mostly pale green with thin brownish edges along its wings. Each wing has a small black and yellowish circle on it. Its front wings spread four or five inches. And each of its hind wings ends in a long, curving tail that makes you think of the sickle shape of a new moon.

The luna's fat caterpillar, too, is soft bluish green with yellow stripes. You could not call it exactly pretty. But at least it does not wear those horned-devil spikes.

This luna larva has a peculiar way of pupating in a cocoon that does not stay where it was built. The cocoon is rather thin and papery, and the caterpillar spins it among tree leaves. Generally it is so poorly fastened that it tumbles to the ground during the autumn.

Some other kinds of moth larvae have the same habit of anchoring their cocoons so lightly that they fall in a short time. Nobody knows the real reason for what seems to us to be just sloppy workmanship.

If you live in the eastern half of the country between

Polyphemus moth

The eyespots of the great polyphemus moth are blue and brown.

Canada and Florida, you have a good chance of seeing lunas. Most of them come out of their cocoons in late spring or early summer. Often the adult moths flutter at night outside brightly lighted windows. And several times I have found them clinging to the leaves of garden flowers or shrubs quite early in the morning. Probably these fellows had emerged from their cocoons only a few hours before.

Two Famous Eyespotters

The polyphemus moth looks very different from a luna. Its velvety body and wings are various shades of soft brown. Each hind wing has an eyespot that is blue and very deep brown. These "eyes" are so large and bright that they seem to be staring right at you. Of course, they are not real eyes, but only fancy markings. The whole moth is even larger than the luna.

Like most of our big moths, polyphemuses never eat and live only a few days. During this time they mate, and the female lays more than 200 creamy white eggs. She usually places these in clusters on the leaves or twigs of a hickory, walnut, elm, oak, maple, beech or some other tree.

In about ten days the baby caterpillars chew their way out of the egg cases and begin to feed. This is the species whose larvae eat eighty-six thousand times their own hatching weight in the first forty-eight hours. After seven weeks or so they are three inches long, which is four thousand times longer than they were when they swallowed their first mouthful of food.

The fully grown larva is a beautiful pale green decorated with silvery lines and some red dots. It is so pleasantly colored that you are sure to be startled when it suddenly raises its forward end and clicks its jaws at you threateningly.

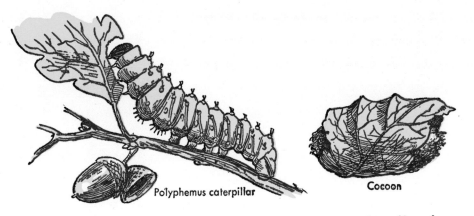

Polyphemus caterpillar

Cocoon

The polyphemus caterpillar pulls a few leaves around itself and fastens them together with silk to make its cocoon.

When this big, stout caterpillar finally stops eating, it wanders around for two or three days looking for a good place to spin a cocoon. At last, having found the right spot, it pulls a few green leaves around itself and fastens them together with silk. Inside this shelter it spins more and more silk, using only a single, unbroken thread which finally may be seven or eight hundred feet long.

Next, the larva produces a liquid which makes a chalky sort of material and binds all the silk threads together. This helps to make the cocoon waterproof. And when all this work has been finished, the caterpillar wriggles out of its own skin and starts turning into a pupa. When the leaves of a polyphemus cocoon shrivel in the fall, the whole thing usually falls to the ground. That is where you may find one any winter day when there is no snow to hide it. It looks like a fat, oval blob with both ends well rounded. Generally it is pale brown and about an inch and a half long. If you hold a "live" one in the palm of your hand, you will be surprised how heavy it feels because of the stout pupa that is inside.

The io moth is another of the species whose cocoons tumble to the ground more often than they stay where the caterpillars built them. Ios are somewhat smaller insects than the luna and polyphemus. But they are more brightly colored than either of these. They are often common from Canada to Florida and west as far as Mexico. They also have many cousins in the tropical parts of the New World. Some of these tropical species have a wingspread of nearly six inches. Naturally they are famous all over the world for their size and beauty.

A male io moth has yellow forewings and red hind ones. In the middle of each rear wing there is one big black and blue eyespot. This is the first thing you notice about the moth when its wings are spread. The two spots side by side look like the glaring eyes of some wild animal. Probably they often help to fool the moth's enemies and perhaps frighten them away.

The female io is marked much like her mate except that her forewings have more red on them. She is bigger than he is, too. A great many other kinds of female moths are larger than the males. This may have something to do with the large number of eggs they lay. Unlaid eggs make insects' bodies heavier, of course. And a heavy body must have good-sized wings to carry it around in the air.

Io larvae will eat the leaves of almost any kind of tree or shrub. They are green with a pinkish white line along each side. This combination of colors often makes them hard to see among green leaves and so helps to protect them against hungry birds and other dangers. But you'd

Io moth

You can recognize the io moth by its big black and blue spots.

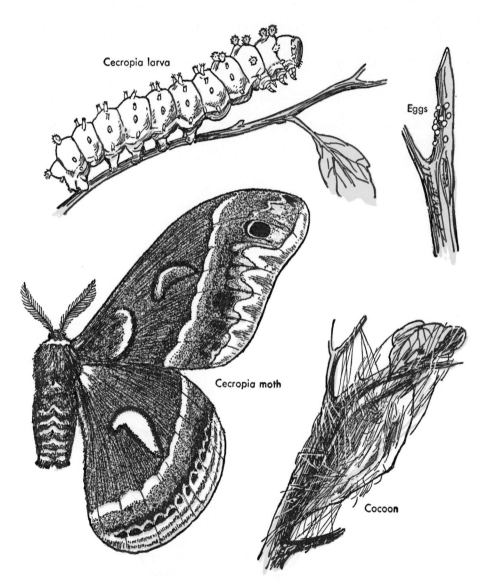

Cecropia larva

Eggs

Cecropia moth

Cocoon

Here you see the four stages of the cecropia moth. Its great wings often measure more than six inches from tip to tip.

better not touch one, because those little tufts of bristles which are sprinkled over it are poisonous and would make your skin itch like fury!

The King-Size Cecropia

If you like moths a good deal larger than our American io, be sure to watch for a cecropia. Its reddish, brown and white wings have no frightening eyespots on them. But they may measure more than six inches from tip to tip. When you see one of these beauties flapping outside a lighted window some early summer evening, it looks big enough to be a bat.

Cecropia moths can be found all up and down our Atlantic Coast and west to the Great Plains. They have no mouths to eat or drink with. But they can get along for nearly a week on the nourishment that was stored up in them while they were caterpillars. This gives them enough time to mate and for the females to lay great numbers of smooth eggs on the twigs or leaves of many different shrubs and trees.

When the larvae first bite their way out of these eggs, they certainly do not look like anything to get excited about. They are so tiny and hairy that it is hard to see them at all. But they grow very fast and have to molt their old skins several times.

In five or six weeks they are several inches long. At this time they are really something to see. Most of the body is green. But the head is black and the three forward pairs of legs are yellow. On the back, right above these legs, are two pairs of coral red knobs with stubby spines on them. Behind these are two more thick yellow knobs, followed by thin yellow ones all the way to the tail end. Finally, the caterpillar has touches of blue scattered here and there.

When one of these gaudy fellows builds its cocoon, it does a first-class job. First, it finds a good tough twig or woody plant stem that stands fairly upright. Then it starts spinning silk around the twig as well as itself. This will keep the little house from falling to the ground like those of the other moths we've been talking about. When the pointed bulging cocoon is finished, it is so firmly fastened to the twig that it may stay there for a year or more after the full-grown moth has crawled out of it.

Inside this outer shell of silk, the caterpillar spins a slightly smaller, well "varnished" home that is absolutely waterproof. Then it molts its larval skin for the last time and is all set for its marvelous transformation into a blackish pupa.

Do you remember my saying that when the time comes for a moth to escape from its cocoon it dissolves the silk at one end and struggles out through the hole? Well, you can see this open hole quite easily in any empty cecropia cocoon. You can often find an old one still fastened to its twig long after its owner has moved out. If you push the point of a very sharp knife or razor blade into the door opening, you can slit the cocoon from end to end. Then you can see just what it is like inside. And down at the bottom you will probably find the shriveled remains of that old pupal coat.

The cocoons spun by promethea caterpillars are even easier to find. They are quite slender, and each one is wrapped inside a leaf which camouflages it beautifully. All winter long they dangle from the twigs of a spice-bush, sassafras, sweet gum or wild cherry tree. It is not hard to spot them after all the other leaves have fallen. Those which have been made into cocoons cannot drop because promethea caterpillars always fasten their stems to the twigs with plenty of silk strands. You will often find several of them hanging in the same tree. I once saw eight in a young wild cherry no taller than my head.

The caterpillars which spin these beautifully made cocoons are bluish green and quite smooth except for four coral red projections near the head. There are some black and yellow dots on them, too.

A female promethea moth looks somewhat like a reddish polyphemus without its eyespots. But the smaller male is quite different. He is very dark brown all over except for the lighter edges of his wings. His feathery antennae are handsome, although they are not as plumelike as those of a polyphemus.

A Famous Silk Maker

I suppose that the most famous moth of all is a fairly small, creamy white one named Bombyx. It lives mostly in China, and its caterpillars eat nothing except the leaves of mulberry trees. They spin all the true silk there is in the world. Experts have calculated that almost two thousand pounds of mulberry leaves must be swallowed to provide a single pound of silk. No wonder many people call these caterpillars silkworms!

Like all moths, these astonishing larvae produce the

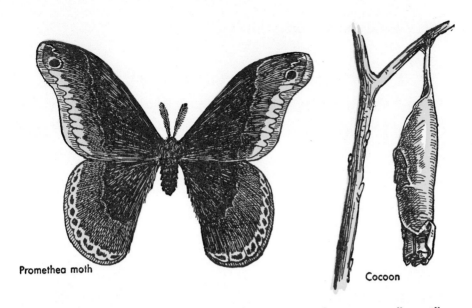

Promethea moth

Cocoon

All winter long the cocoon spun by a promethea caterpillar will dangle from the twig of a sweet gum or wild cherry tree.

silk-making liquid inside their heads. It comes out through tiny spinnerets in their upper lips, just as it does from other caterpillars. One of them can make a thousand feet of silk thread in about thirty-three working hours. And there will not be a knot or even a kink anywhere in it.

The caterpillars use most of this silk for building their cocoons. In order to make silk threads for human use, people collect the cocoons soon after they have been completed. Then they soak them in hot water until the pupae inside are dead. Next, the long strands of silk are very carefully unwound by hand. And last, many separate strands are spun together so as to make the silk threads which are finally woven into beautiful shimmering cloth. It sometimes takes 25,000 cocoons to produce one pound of finished silk.

Moths With Birds' Names

Toward evening on some clear spring or summer day you may see a small, reddish moth buzzing from one garden flower to another. Its wings beat so fast that they are just a blur. It has a marvelous way of "standing still" in the air for a moment in front of one flower before moving on to the next. And at the rear end of its very stout body there is a tuft of fuzz that makes you think of a stumpy little tail.

This busy small fellow looks so much like a hummingbird that it has been given the name of hummingbird moth. Many people call it the hummingbird clearwing because its pointed, rather narrow wings are transparent in the middle. Its feeding tongue is as long as its body. And it is quite common anywhere from Canada to Florida and as far west as the Mississippi River.

The caterpillar of a hummingbird moth is green with

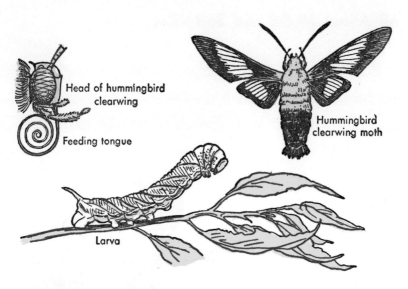

The tongue of the hummingbird clearwing moth is very long.

slanting whitish lines on both sides. Most of its skin is quite rough and wrinkled. At its rear end there is a long, curving red "horn" that reminds you of a dog's tail.

There are several species of hummingbird clearwings in North America north of Mexico. When one of their larvae is full-grown and ready to turn into a pupa, it simply crawls under some fallen leaves and spins a thin cocoon right on the ground.

All hummingbird moths belong to a large tribe known as hawk moths or sphinxes. The scientific name for this big family is Sphyngidae. This Latin title means "like a sphinx." And here is the reason why it was given to them:

All About Moths and Butterflies

When one of their caterpillars takes a rest, it raises the forward half of its body into the air and arches its neck. This makes it look somewhat like that gigantic old figure of the sphinx in the Egyptian desert.

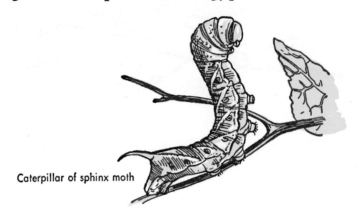

Caterpillar of sphinx moth

Hawk moths are found in nearly all parts of the world. Some of the African species have a wingspread of only about an inch. But in our country most sorts are two, three or four inches from tip to tip. All of them are astonishingly strong and fast fliers. Their stiff, pointed wings look as if they were especially built for speed. And the body, particularly where they join it, is also thick and sturdy.

One of the biggest and most common species is the tomato hawk moth or tomato sphinx. Its mottled brown and gray wings have a spread of four to five inches, and there are yellow spots on the sides of its abdomen. It is found all over North and South America.

The caterpillar of this species is a real whopper— three or four inches long and very stout, too. Its appetite for the leaves of tomato, eggplant, pepper, potato and related plants is terrific. It eats so much that it often seriously damages the crops grown by gardeners and farmers.

When this greedy caterpillar is fully grown, it burrows into the ground for three or four inches and turns into a strange-looking pupa. Most pupae, as you know, have a hard outer case that is all in one piece, as you might say. But a tomato sphinx moth has a very long proboscis, and there must be extra space for this to grow in during the pupal stage. For this reason every tomato sphinx pupa has a special outside tongue case that curves down from one end like the handle on a pitcher.

Female tomato hawk moths lay their eggs on the undersides of leaves. These hatch in a week, and then the fun begins! The caterpillars eat so much and so fast that they are full-grown in three or four weeks. During this short time they outgrow five different skins and have to put on bigger ones.

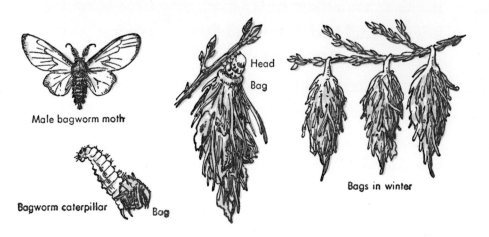

Male bagworm moth

Bagworm caterpillar

Bag

Head

Bag

Bags in winter

The bagworm caterpillar spends the winter in its rough "bag."

Some Marvelous Midgets

Medium-size and large moths, such as these species you have been reading about, are only a small part of the whole moth group. There are many thousands of really little ones, some of which have a wingspread of only half an inch. Most of these are brownish or grayish and not especially good-looking. They fairly swarm around outdoor porch lights and at lighted windows on any clear summer or early autumn night. Most people just call them "millers" and let it go at that.

Some of these miniature characters, though, are every bit as astonishing as the big species. They have different shapes and colors, different ways of eating, living and growing up. Many of them do not even look like moths. When you know something about them you will have a much better idea of how unbelievable the moth branch of the Order Lepidoptera actually is.

Take the bagworm, for instance. It is very common from our Atlantic Coast westward to the Great Plains. And when you hear how it lives, you will agree that it is one of the queerest of all insects.

When a black-and-white bagworm caterpillar hatches in the spring, it is only one-eighth of an inch long. Also, it has no legs except the usual three pairs near its front end.

As this little creature starts feeding on the leaves of the plant where it hatched, it scrambles around on these front legs with the rest of its body sticking up in the air. It also spins silk which it uses to hold bits of bark and other plant scraps together in a ring around its forward end. As the larva grows, this ring is extended backward until it forms a complete house or "bag" from one to two inches long.

The caterpillar lives inside this home and carries it everywhere. The only part of the little fellow that ever comes outside is its forward end where the head, mouth and legs are. And when it stops to eat, it fastens the bag to a twig with bits of silk while it enjoys the meal.

By late summer the bagworm larvae have molted four times and are a little less than an inch long. It is now time for them to pupate, so each one of them fastens its bag firmly to a twig with silk. Inside this tough, shaggy shelter it turns into a chrysalis for the winter. You often see these queer cocoons dangling from many kinds of trees in the Atlantic states from Massachusetts to Florida and as far west as Texas.

When spring comes, the adult moths emerge from their pupal cases. The males have black, furry bodies and their almost transparent wings spread to about an inch. They get out at the lower ends of the bags. Then they fly around looking for the females. But these females have no wings at all and never come out of their bags.

Mating takes place inside the female's home. Then she lays five hundred or more eggs in the upper part of her bag. When this has been done, she packs scales from her own body in the bottom of the bag and quickly dies. Later in the spring the eggs hatch, and immediately the hundreds of new little caterpillars creep out of the bag and start making their portable homes.

A Dainty Speed Demon

Bagworm moths are not the only small ones that do amazing things. The peach tree borer is almost as hard to believe. This species looks something like a wasp. Of course it is not one, and it has no sting. Its wings spread about an inch and a half.

The female is blue-black and wears a bright orange belt around the middle of her abdomen. The male is more brownish and wears several yellow belts. Both males and females have partly transparent wings with which they fly very strongly and in broad daylight. You can find them all over the United States east of the Rocky Mountains, and they have lots of cousins in California.

About the middle of summer each female lays several hundred eggs near the base of a peach tree. These hatch in ten days, and the first thing the little white caterpillars do is to start chewing or "boring" their way into the tree's bark.

Once they get through the bark, the young larvae

feed on the soft wood just underneath. Some of them even chew downward to the roots and continue eating there. All of them spend the winter in their burrows and eat some more in the spring. When they are about an inch long, they come out and pupate in silk cocoons spun underground near the foot of the tree. By midsummer the new moths are out of their cocoons, and the females begin the job of laying a whole new generation of eggs.

Peach-tree borers kill many thousands of trees every year. You see, the larvae eat so much of the soft inner wood that the sap cannot get through to the upper parts of the tree. Of course, no tree can live unless plenty of sap reaches all of its branches, twigs and leaves during the growing season.

Another of these peculiar wasplike moths whose caterpillars grow up inside plants is known as the squash borer. Its larvae often kill squash, pumpkin, gourd, cucumber and even muskmelon and cantaloupe vines. They have such big appetites that gardeners and farmers all the way from New England to Argentina, in South America, do everything they can to get rid of them. If you measure a good map of the Western

Hemisphere, you will find that this is a distance of more than four thousand miles.

The mother of a squash borer has fringes on her hind legs that make her look as if she is wearing long pants. Her mate has these, too. He also wears "short pants" fringes on his middle pair of legs. Both parents have transparent hind wings, and their general color is coppery green in front and red behind.

This little fancy-dress moth flies around in the daytime and lays an egg here and there on the main stems and leaf stalks of her favorite vines. By the time she gets through with this, she has placed a hundred and fifty or two hundred eggs exactly where she wants them to be. Then her job is finished, and she dies.

In about a week the eggs hatch; and the tiny white, brown-headed larvae tunnel into the center of the stems. There they keep moving slowly forward, eating as they

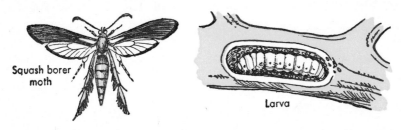

Squash borer moth

Larva

The larva of the squash borer tunnels into a plant stem.

go. In four or five weeks they are fully grown and probably an inch long.

It is now time for them to come out, burrow a couple of inches into the ground, and pupate inside cocoons. Before these cocoons have been finished, the vine is either badly withered or completely dead. It is hard to believe that a handful of small caterpillars, feeding where nobody can see them, can kill so many yards of a strong, wide-spreading vine like a squash.

These two tiny moths look about as different from the Isabella tiger moth as any insect could be. The Isabella is much more like a regular moth, for its body is thick and its yellow wings are marked by scattered reddish spots. It is really pretty, although it measures less than two inches from tip to tip.

The Good-Natured Woolly Bears

The really famous members of this Isabella species, however, are the caterpillars. If you have lived in the rural parts of the United States, you have probably seen them. They are those furry, black-and-brown fellows that go crawling across roads and all kinds of open places in the warm autumn sunshine. When you pick them up, they curl into balls like hedgehogs and lie perfectly still. Most people call them banded woolly bears. And there is an old country belief that when the brown bands around their middles are narrow and the black ones at the ends are wide there is going to be a long, cold winter.

You are not likely to see many woolly bears in the summer when they are feeding quietly on grass, weeds and other soft-leaf plants near the ground. But early in the fall they stop eating and travel around looking for good spots to spend the winter. At this time they seem to be everywhere. You notice them especially on driveways, sidewalks, around houses and sheds, on stone walls and fence posts.

The winter home of these amusing caterpillars is some quiet, sheltered spot which is dark, dry and free of snow. They particularly like to crawl under big flat rocks, into loose walls or piles of dead leaves, woodpiles and among pieces of boards under a roof. When they find what they are after, they do not spin a cocoon. Instead, they simply curl up snugly and go into a sort of deep sleep, called hibernation.

With the return of warm spring weather, the woolly

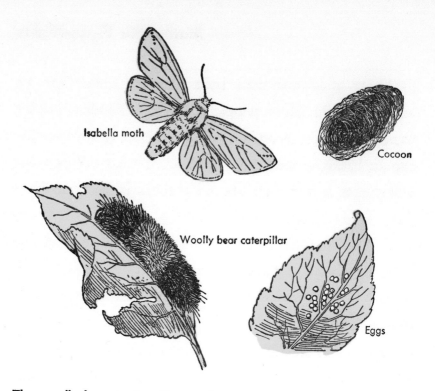

Isabella moth

Cocoon

Woolly bear caterpillar

Eggs

The woolly bear caterpillar makes a neat cocoon in the spring, and out of this comes the Isabella moth.

bear wakes up and makes a neat oval cocoon out of silk mixed with its own hair. Inside this it becomes a pupa, and finally emerges as the Isabella moth whose yellow eggs are always clustered on the lower sides of leaves.

Woolly bears are a lot of fun to have around. You will soon find that they are good-natured, perfectly harmless, and rather pretty in their fat, furry way. They have been special favorites of mine for a long time.

There is a great difference between these friendly, fur-coated clowns and the unpleasant characters known as red-humped caterpillars. For one thing, a woolly bear usually lives by itself. But when you see a red-humped caterpillar, it is sure to be just one of a closely crowded gang of maybe two or three dozen. Also, the red-hump is an ugly yellow color streaked with brown and white. It has a red head and a red swelling on its back, and it wears twenty-four sharp black spines. Yes, it looks mean and acts mean when you frighten it, and it raises its front end into the air as if it were ready for a fight.

These red-humped caterpillars are only about an inch long when they have grown up. But they have enormous appetites for the leaves of a great many kinds of trees. A few gangs of them in a small tree often strip all the leaves off several of the branches.

Red-humps have a special fondness for fruit trees, birches, hickories and walnuts. Everyone who likes the country is glad when they quit feeding and go into the ground or under trash to spend the winter as pupae inside thin cocoons.

You might expect that such disagreeable larvae would have ugly mothers. But the female moths which lay the masses of eggs from which they hatch are decidedly pretty. Their brownish wings are marked with gray, and spread to about an inch and a half. The bodies are grayish, too. And there are short fringes along their antennae and hind legs. Altogether, they look as harmless as any moths you ever saw.

Hide Those Wings!

The soft markings of these quiet little moths are one form of protective coloration, of course. Indeed, practically all moth species have some kind of system to make their lives safer. There is one big group of them, called the underwings, whose markings help them in *two* ways to escape from their enemies. These surprising insects are also known as Catocalas, and there are more than a hundred kinds of them here in North America.

An underwing moth's rear wings are colored differently from the forward pair. In some of the larger species they are almost black. But usually they are yellow and black, red and black, or some other strong combination. The front wings, however, are mixed brown and gray, and so softly marked that they are hard to see.

The showy hind wings of these moths are very no-

Underwing moth

The showy hind wings of the underwing moth are carefully hidden when it lights on a branch or tree trunk.

ticeable when their owner flies. They would be the first thing to attract the attention of a hungry whip-poor-will or some other bird. Such an enemy might easily decide to catch that moth if it could. So it takes off in pursuit, its own eyes fixed on those showy, easily seen wings. This sounds bad for the Catocala. But wait a minute!

A frightened Catocala seldom flies far. It generally lights on the first branch, stump or tree trunk it comes to. And the moment it stops, it folds its bark-colored fore wings over the smaller, stronger-colored hind ones so as to cover them completely. The change in appearance is so sudden that the pursuer must think the whole moth has vanished into thin air. Besides this, the camouflage is now amazingly perfect. It is easy to guess how puzzled any enemy would be by such an unexpected disappearance.

All of the underwings are well worth watching for. When you see a moth whose front wings are so mottled or streaked that they look like the gray-brown bark of a tree, it may belong to this interesting group. If its hind wings are strongly barred with black and red, or black and yellow, the chances are that it is one of them. So study the markings of the little underwing in the picture, and then keep your eyes open for a real live one.

There is a much smaller moth whose bright rear wings are hidden by the dull forward ones when the insect is at rest. But it is not a true underwing. Its name is codling moth. And every year its pinkish larvae, which are called apple worms, ruin many thousands of tons of apples in all parts of the world. If you have ever started to eat a good-looking apple and found that its whole center was brown and squashy, just blame it on the codling moth. The insect's name comes from the old European word "codlin," which means a small, young apple.

This little fruit-eater is oddly marked. Its front wings are dark brown with lighter bars wiggling across them. The whole body and the *fringed* hind wings are reddish orange. And when it lights and quickly folds its forward wings over the rear ones, it is only a quarter of an inch long.

Codling moths come out of their cocoons about the time that apple blossoms are opening. As soon as the petals have spread wide, the females fly to these flowers and lay tiny white eggs on the nearby twigs and leaves. These hatch in from one to three weeks, and the little larvae crawl at once to the nearest baby apples.

Almost before you know it, the caterpillars have chewed their way through what is left of the flower (the little withered bunch that is on the opposite side of the apple from the stem) and are burrowing toward the center of the fruit. When they are an inch long, they tunnel out again through the side of the apple and spin their cocoons under bits of loose bark on the branches or trunk of the tree.

All About Moths and Butterflies

Most moth larvae, as you know, begin to change into their pupal stage as soon as their cocoons are finished. But codling moths have their own special ways of behaving. They do not change to pupae until the following spring. Then it takes another few weeks for the adult moths to be formed, crawl out, and start hiding themselves as soon as they light on something!

A Shelter Tent for the Gang

When you have watched moths and butterflies for a while, you will begin to wonder if there is any limit to their peculiar habits. Each species seems to do things a little differently from the rest. And when you come to the tent caterpillar, you will agree that its life is *very* different.

Tent caterpillar moths are fuzzy, light brown little fellows with white stripes on their front wings. There are several species of them in different parts of the United States and Canada.

During the summer each female lays a broad belt of eggs around a twig. Then she covers the belt with a sticky fluid which hardens quickly and looks like shiny

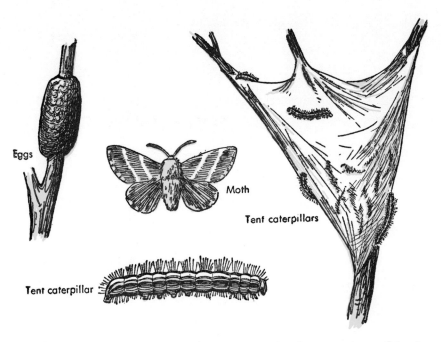

Eggs

Moth

Tent caterpillars

Tent caterpillar

At night the baby caterpillars stay inside the waterproof tent.

brown varnish. She often chooses apple trees or wild cherry trees for her egg laying. This is because the leaves of these trees start to grow early in the season and are favorite foods of the larvae.

All through the fall and winter these strange egg bands stick tightly to their twigs. Finally, in the very early spring, the little blackish larvae hatch. As soon as they are out of the eggs, they head for the nearest branch or twig fork and start spinning a silk "tent."

On pleasant days the whole gang of baby caterpillars

feeds on the tree's leaves which are just beginning to appear. At night and in rainy weather they stay inside their waterproof tent. You can almost see them grow. And as they get bigger and bigger, they spin more and more silk to make the tent larger. In four or five weeks the caterpillars are two inches long, and the tent may measure more than a foot from side to side.

By this time many of the tree's leaves have been completely eaten away. So the larvae crawl down the trunk and go wandering around looking for spots to spin cocoons and change into pupae. You often see them creeping on tree trunks and the sides of houses. These are favorite places for attaching their rather flat, dirty white cocoons. Within the next three or four weeks, the young moths will come out and start laying a new crop of egg belts for next spring's hatching.

Here is another peculiar fact about tent caterpillars. Their numbers rise and fall according to a rather regular pattern. For five years they become more and more plentiful until there are countless millions of them. Then you will see fewer and fewer for another five years. And five years after that there will again be great crowds of them.

The reason why the tent caterpillar population goes up and down in this way is somewhat puzzling. Probably it is because some insect enemy which feeds on them increases along with the caterpillars and finally gets the best of them. Then, of course, the little tent builders will become fewer until almost all their enemies die of starvation. Once this happens, the caterpillars can start building up their numbers for another comeback.

Strange Uses for Silk

Tent caterpillars would be very badly out of luck if they could not spin lots and lots of silk. And so would the larvae of another little moth that use their silk in a very different way. One name for these peculiar fellows is fall cankerworms. However, most people call them inchworms, measuring worms, or loopers because of the odd way they move around. They are common in the United States from the Atlantic to the Pacific.

Cankerworm mothers have no wings, but how they do crawl! They are gray, buglike, and about half an inch long. The males are grayish and much prettier, with a wingspread of perhaps an inch.

All About Moths and Butterflies

The adult moths come out of their underground cocoons in the autumn after the thermometer has gone below freezing. They are almost the only species with such an apparently crazy habit. Immediately the females start creeping up tree trunks and out along the branches and twigs. As they go, they lay masses of grayish eggs on the bark. As soon as they finish this they die, and that's that!

All winter long those unprotected eggs stick to their places no matter how cold and stormy the weather is. Their only enemies seem to be the chickadees and other small wild birds which thoroughly enjoy eating tiny raw, cold eggs. In the spring, about the time the trees' leaves begin to come out, the eggs hatch. From each one comes a brown and white caterpillar with pale stripes along its sides.

As soon as these little larvae start going somewhere, you can see why they are called measuring worms. Instead of crawling along steadily like most caterpillars, they begin by hunching their backs so as to pull their hind legs forward until they are just behind the front ones. Then they stand on their hind legs with most of their bodies raised high into the air.

A measuring worm can stand on its hind legs and reach into the air.

For several seconds these straight, elevated bodies waver this way and that. They are really uncertain where to go next! Finally the front end comes down, and the forward legs take hold of the leaf or twig far ahead of the hind legs. As soon as they get a good grip, the hind legs let go and the body humps into a high loop which brings them forward until they are again close behind the front ones. The caterpillar is now all set to repeat its reaching-out stunt. The whole performance looks as though the creature were measuring a line inch by inch.

Now about the silk-using part of this strange story:

The larvae feed on the tree's leaves, of course. And as they grow larger each one of them sometimes fastens a silk thread to the leaf where it is eating. Next, it stops chewing, lets go with its legs and drops toward the ground, paying out more silk as it goes. At last it stops making the thread and swings around in the air for a few minutes. Then it climbs back up its silken life line and continues its meal as if nothing unusual had happened.

Why do these little caterpillars perform such astonishing acrobatics? I'm not sure. Maybe they are just practicing for the future. You see, when they are fully grown many of them will use these silk threads to reach the ground. There they will spin cocoons and pupate. Besides this, when they dangle on their long lines on windy days, some of them may be blown far away from their home tree. This happens year after year. The result is that the small loopers keep spreading over a larger and larger area. Such traveling is especially important, of course, for a species whose females cannot fly even a single stroke!

When a Flower Needs a Friend

Measuring worms and other moths are surely queer creatures. But it has always seemed to me that the habits of the yucca moth are the most astonishing of all. In fact, so far as I know, not a single other member of the whole moth group behaves like this strange, snow-white midget, or even lives the way it does.

Yuccas are mostly desert plants. They have stiff, pointed leaves and white blossoms that hang like bells from tall stalks. Yucca moths could not live without these flowers. And without these moths, yucca plants could not produce any seeds!

Here is the way this remarkable arrangement works:

Yucca moths, of which there are several species, are only a quarter of an inch long. They fly at night and hide in the blossoms during the day. It is very difficult to see them because of their small size and the way their color matches that of the flowers.

These little insects have two special extensions on their mouths. With these the female moth gathers yucca pollen and shapes it into a ball that may be as big as her head. Then she places the ball firmly on the stigma, or pistil, of the flower. This is the part of the blossom which must be fertilized in order to form seeds. Such *pollination*, as it is called, is often done accidentally by various insects on many other kinds of flowers. But the yucca moth is the only species that does it on purpose.

After she has pollinated a stigma, the moth lays a few eggs in the lower part of the blossom. When the seed-bearing fruit has begun to form, larvae hatch from the eggs. They are almost too small to see, but immediately these mites bore into the fruit and start feeding on its pulp. Generally they eat some of the baby seeds, too. But a few seeds are sure to live long enough to ripen.

Finally, when the fruit falls to the ground, two things happen. First, the uneaten seeds have a chance to sprout and grow into new yucca plants. And second, the full-grown larvae burrow into the ground and pupate there for the winter. Next year the adult moths will come out of their cocoons at the same time that a new crop of yucca flowers is ready to be pollinated.

Yuccas of one kind or another are grown in flower gardens in many parts of the country. If you look very carefully into the centers of their fully opened blossoms, you may spot a few of these wee, pure white moths with their wings folded down along their backs. And when the fruits have fallen, cut them open and perhaps you will find a little larva finishing its dinner inside.

Butterfly Days and Ways

Swallowtails for Surprises

Butterflies, as well as moths and many thousands of other wild creatures and plants, have two kinds of names. The most puzzling ones are the scientific names. These are always written in Latin. They are used mostly by scientists because they are very exact and are the same in all countries. The other kind is the "common" names, such as you find in this book. They are written in the language of the country in which they are commonly used. Often a wild creature has several common names in different countries and even in different parts of the same country.

In most cases the scientific as well as the common names have something to do with the creature's appearance or habits. A good example of this is the swallowtail tribe of butterflies. Many of these handsome insects have streamers on their hind wings which remind you of the long, forked tails of certain swallows. There are about thirty species of them in North America north of Mexico.

The largest of all swallowtails are found in the tropical islands of the Far East. One group of them, often called "bird-wing butterflies," are particularly brilliant in color. Sometimes their wings spread to a full nine inches. One of these giants, which has been named Victoria after the famous Queen of England, has a wing-spread of nearly ten inches. And another swallowtail, found in Africa, measures twelve inches from tip to tip. This may be the largest butterfly in the world.

The tiger swallowtail is one of the biggest and show-iest members of its group here in our own country. You are likely to see it almost anywhere from Canada to the Gulf of Mexico and from the Atlantic to the Rocky Mountains.

Tiger swallowtail
butterfly

The yellow and black wings of a tiger swallowtail often measure
more than six inches across.

All About Moths and Butterflies

This species was the first American butterfly that ever had its picture painted. That happened almost four hundred years ago. And the painter was John White, the Governor of Sir Walter Raleigh's third colony on Roanoke Island, in North Carolina.

Tiger swallowtail is a good name for this butterfly, for its "tailed" yellow wings are striped and edged with black in a way that makes you think of the markings on a regular four-footed tiger. They are big wings, too, measuring four to six and a half inches from tip to tip. The smaller hind wings have small blue, red and yellow markings in their mostly black edgings. It is a strange fact that most of the female "tigers" in the South are dark brown all over.

These splendid butterflies behave as if they know how handsome they are. They fly strongly and often sail on motionless wings across sunny places where their colors show most brightly. One of the best places to watch for them is in the flower garden, especially when lilies are in bloom. On pleasant early summer days you often see them flitting around the tops of tall woodland and lawn trees where there are plenty of leaves but no blossoms at all. I often wonder what it is that interests them away up there. But I have never found the full answer to the puzzle.

Another peculiar thing about tiger swallowtails is their habit of visiting mud puddles and gathering around some creature that has been dead long enough to have a very strong smell. It is still more surprising to learn from a great authority on butterflies that these big fellows are attracted by the smell of cigar smoke.

There is a very different looking swallowtail in our Central States and southward to Florida and the Gulf of Mexico. It is called the zebra swallowtail because of the shape and color of its markings. The wings are dark brown, and the stripes across them are almost white. The "tails" on the rear wings are much longer than the tiger's, too. This species is particularly common where papaws grow, for the leaves of these trees are the favorite food of its caterpillars.

You naturally expect all the butterflies of any particular species to look alike. But zebra swallowtails would fool you on this. Adults that come out of their pupal cases in early spring have short "tails" and short wings. There is a great deal of white on them. Others that emerge in late spring have longer wings and broader,

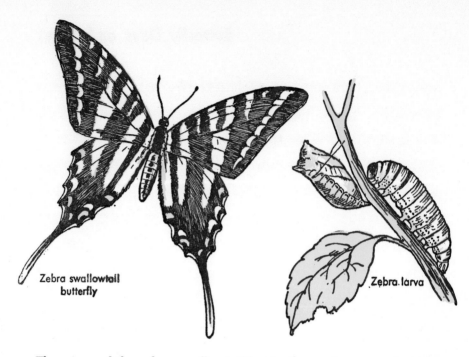

Zebra swallowtail
butterfly

Zebra. larva

The wings of the zebra swallowtail butterfly are brown and white.

darker markings. And those which start flying in the summer are the biggest and darkest of all.

Nobody seems to know the real reason for these differences. It may be that the temperature has something to do with them.

Speaking of dark colors, have you ever seen the black swallowtail? It is quite different from the two kinds we have been talking about, for its black wings have no stripes of any kind. Instead, there are rows of rather small yellow spots on them, and another row of blue spots. The wingspread is only two and a half to three and a half inches. But this butterfly is common over practically all of North America except the Far North, and it certainly is worth watching for.

The still darker spicebush swallowtail is a stylish looking fellow, too. It likes flower gardens and woods even better than the black one does. And in some sections it is more common.

The larvae of these four swallowtails are as different from each other as their parents are. A tiger caterpillar is smooth and green, with a pair of orange and black eyespots on its "shoulders." It lives in trees where it builds a sheltering roof over itself by folding down the edges of a leaf. And its rough brown chrysalis, or pupal case, is mottled with green. Dr. A. B. Comstock, a famous insect authority, once saw two tiger larvae butting each other like a couple of goats. Finally they stopped this strange battle and crawled away in opposite directions.

Zebra larvae are greenish, too, but they have no eyespots at all. Before they turn into pupae, they often eat some of their brothers and sisters.

The chrysalises of the zebra are really pretty. Instead of being rough and brown, they are a lovely green and there isn't a rough spot on them. A few thin, reddish and yellowish lines and dots make them still more attractive.

Caterpillars of the black swallowtail have no eyespots to fool enemies, as their tiger cousins do. But their green skins are handsomely decorated with black and yellow bands. These markings probably help to camouflage them while they are feeding. Many people call them celery caterpillars because the leaves of this popular vegetable are one of their best-liked foods.

And what about the caterpillars of the spicebush swallowtail? Well, they also are green and yellow, but they wear *two* terrific pairs of eyespots that could startle anybody or anything!

All our American swallowtails are alike in two odd ways. First, their caterpillars have yellow or orange scent organs hidden just behind their heads. When the caterpillar is disturbed, it thrusts out these forked "horns" which give off a sickening smell. One good whiff of it will prove to you that these little gadgets are an excellent method of self-defense.

The second likeness between our swallowtails is this: When their caterpillars are ready to pupate, they fasten their tail ends to twigs or stems with silk. And, as if to make doubly sure that they won't fall, they also put strong silk threads around their "shoulders" and fasten both ends to the same twigs.

A Hungry Immigrant

In this country, probably more damage is done to farm and garden crops by the larvae of moths than by butterfly caterpillars. But when it comes to the white European cabbage butterfly, you do have a very serious troublemaker.

This species reached North America almost a century ago. And here is a list of the cultivated plants its caterpillars eat: broccoli, beets, Brussels sprouts, cabbage, cauliflower, celery, collards, horseradish, lettuce, kale, kohlrabi, mustard, parsley, peas, potatoes, radishes, turnips, tomatoes and water cress. So you see they have a healthy appetite.

These downy, green, awfully hungry caterpillars are only a little over an inch long when fully grown. You would expect them to be fat. But actually they are quite slim. At least three huge broods of them hatch out of greenish white eggs every season. It is no wonder they are common all over the country.

The adult cabbage butterflies have white wings that spread about two inches. The tip of each front one is dark gray, and a little below this is one small black dot —or two of them in the case of a female. The undersides of the rear wings are yellowish.

Of all the butterflies in the United States, this is the one you see most frequently. From spring until fall you find them in all kinds of open places in the country, in villages and towns, even in the parks and streets of our

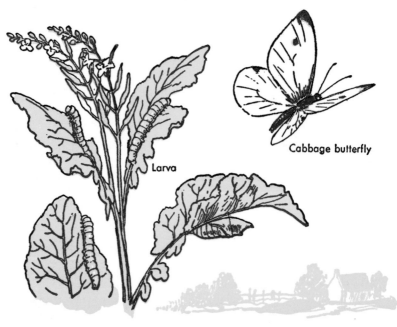

Larva

Cabbage butterfly

From spring until fall you can see the lovely cabbage butterfly.

largest cities. They are tough fellows, too. Last year, in a field behind our house in Connecticut, I saw one flying cheerfully around late in November.

Not all butterflies like to live in the wide open spaces the way the cabbage butterfly does. In fact, some kinds would much rather stay where sunlight seldom reaches them.

One of the prettiest of these shade-lovers is the little wood satyr. It is colored with lovely soft browns and has two black eyespots on each wing. When flying, it measures about an inch and a half across.

This little beauty is one of six or seven closely related species. It is fairly common in the eastern half of North America from Canada to the Gulf States. And there are a great many more of its cousins in the tropics.

Wood satyrs behave differently from most butterflies. They fly slowly and quite near the ground. Sometimes they even walk around among the fallen leaves, like beetles. You would think it would be easy to catch them. But they are experts at getting away by flying right through tall grass and thick bushes where you cannot see them.

I have never discovered just how they do this. Ap-

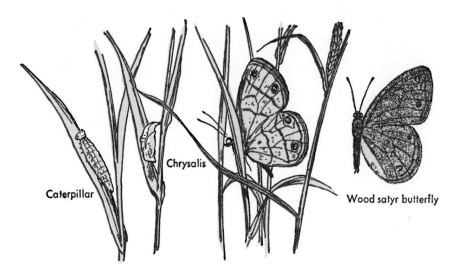

Caterpillar

Chrysalis

Wood satyr butterfly

Wood satyrs fly easily through tall grass and thick bushes.

parently they hold their wings together above their backs most of the time. Of course this makes them so thin that they can slip through very narrow openings between the crowded stems. But where do they get the push needed to send them forward? Does it come from those occasional short flips of their wings, which look like only the start of a real stroke? Or do they use their legs in some invisible way? It is a real puzzle! Maybe you can solve it someday by carefully watching a little wood satyr working its way through the thick growths it likes so much.

The caterpillar of a wood satyr lives among grasses

and eats them, too. He is even harder to see than his parents, for his color is a greenish brown that matches his surroundings perfectly. And the chrysalis inside which he turns into a butterfly is also perfectly camouflaged. It is pale brown and hangs upside down from a bit of silk fastened to a grass stem.

Some Feet Are Like Brushes

Some members of the largest family of true butterflies are called brush-footed. That is because their front legs are very short and often so hairy that they look like brushes. Many of our common kinds belong to this tremendous group. And you could not ask for more interesting and beautiful insects anywhere.

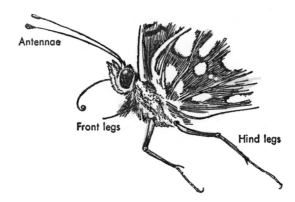

This close-up shows the short hairy front legs of what is known as the brush-footed butterfly.

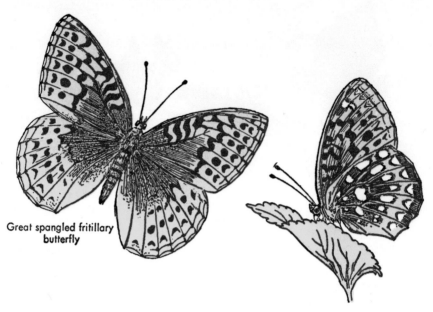

As a butterfly, the great spangled fritillary is bold and showy.

One of these peculiar butterflies is called the silver-spot, or great spangled fritillary. Its shaded, yellowish brown wings are handsomely dotted and waved with black. They have a spread of more than three inches. And the undersides of the rear ones are decorated with many spots that gleam like silver.

You may find this showy, fast-flying butterfly almost anywhere from Nova Scotia to the Georgia mountains and westward to Oklahoma and Arkansas. The best places to look for it are wet meadows, roadsides and sunny flower gardens. It is actively on the wing from

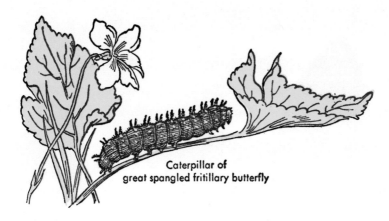

Caterpillar of
great spangled fritillary butterfly

As a caterpillar it hides all day, moving only at night.

the middle of spring until October. And it sips the nectar from many different kinds of blossoms.

It seems strange that such a free-moving, out-in-the-open butterfly should be remarkably shy during its caterpillar stage. Such a difference just does not make sense. But, as far as we know, silverspot larvae hide all day and move around only at night. Apparently their only food is various kinds of violets. Also, they hibernate as soon as they come out of the yellow eggs, and eat nothing at all until the following spring.

A fully grown silverspot caterpillar is not exactly neat looking. As a matter of fact, it is dark reddish brown, and it bristles with branching black spines. I don't believe the strangely shaped brown chrysalis could ever win a beauty prize, either.

Another familiar butterfly is the painted lady. If this sounds like an unusually fancy name for a butterfly, just wait until you see one with its red, black and white spotted wings spread wide in the bright sunshine!

This very common species is about an inch smaller than the silverspot. It is found in nearly all parts of the world except the Arctic and the Antarctic. Here in the United States and Canada there must be billions of painted ladies during some years. When they are especially numerous, a great many of them migrate southward. It may be that they do this because they need more space in which to live.

Painted ladies like all kinds of open places where there is plenty of light. You will find them in sunny swamps, on mountain tops, and just about everywhere in between. They are swift, strong fliers and feed on many kinds of flowers. Their special favorites, though, are thistles. They like the blossoms of these prickly plants so much that many people call them thistle butterflies. Another good name for them would be "touch-and-go butterflies," because they are restless and seldom stay long in any one spot. Sometimes the adults hibernate in hidden nooks all winter and come out again in the spring.

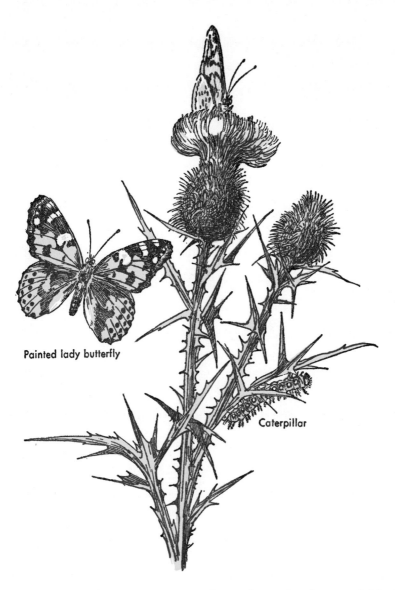

Painted lady butterfly

Caterpillar

The painted lady gets its name from the red, white and black
spotted wings. Its caterpillar is green and white.

A painted lady caterpillar is a rather pretty mixture of green and yellow. But you would hardly call it handsome, for its back is covered with spines and its head is so fuzzy that it looks as though it needs a haircut.

Pearl crescents, another brush-footed kind, are about the same size as painted ladies. But they are always ready to fight other butterflies much larger than themselves. Perhaps they just like to keep everything for themselves. Most of these battles are in the air, and the speed of the crescents' dives, twists and turns almost makes you dizzy. Sometimes the little warriors go so fast on their yellow and brown wings that you lose sight of them for a moment.

The larvae of these speedy little fellows are dark brown and covered with black bristles. The only bright things about them are some yellow spots.

As I have said, the pearl crescent caterpillar is not good-looking. But when you see the larvae of a viceroy, another of the brush-footed clan, you will really stare. This blotchy gray and yellow caterpillar is fat and bumpy, and it has four camel-like humps on its back. Two straight brown "horns" sticking up from the largest hump give it a comically startled expression. At a quick glance the whole caterpillar could easily be mistaken for an old broken dead leaf. This camouflage probably helps to keep enemies from noticing it. The fact that it feeds mostly at night and remains hidden during the day must often save its life, too.

As soon as these homely youngsters hatch in the autumn, they eat a little and then start building the strangest winter homes you can imagine. Here is how they do it:

Each little caterpillar eats away the outer half of its particular leaf except for the stiff central rib. The inner half, nearest the twig from which the leaf grows, is only

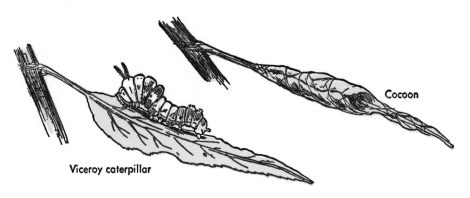

Viceroy caterpillar

Cocoon

The viceroy caterpillar makes its cocoon from part of a leaf.

slightly eaten along its edges. Then the caterpillar fastens the central rib to the twig with plenty of silk, so that winter winds cannot blow it down. And finally it rolls the remaining sides of the leaf into a tube, lines this with more silk, and is all set to hibernate inside the shelter.

In the spring the larva wakes up when the new leaves start to come out. These supply plenty of fresh food for it to grow on, turn into a chrysalis, and finally become a butterfly.

Perhaps you wonder how a mere scrap of a caterpillar like this can live through bitter cold with only a piece of dead leaf and some silk to protect it. This is the almost incredible answer:

During the late autumn most of the water inside the larva's body was used for making important chemical changes. Finally this water became so loaded with dissolved substances that it could not possibly freeze even in sub-zero weather. It is a little like our way of protecting a car's cooling system against the cold by pouring antifreeze into the radiator.

An adult viceroy butterfly looks stunning in its bold, orange-brown and black wing pattern. It resembles a

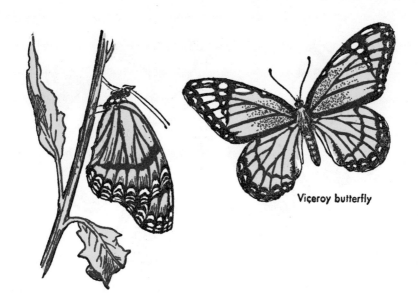

The wings of a viceroy are bold orange-brown and black.

small monarch butterfly so closely that it could easily be mistaken for one. Scientists think that this imitation often saves the viceroy's life. The monarch, you see, has such a bitter taste that many birds and other creatures have learned not to eat it. A viceroy, on the other hand, tastes all right to a bird and is perfectly good eating. But anything that has once bitten into a monarch is likely to leave the viceroy alone for fear of getting into the same sort of taste trouble that it did with the monarch.

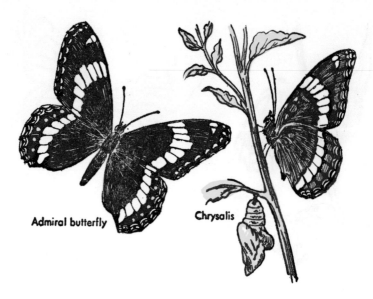

The admiral butterfly is a gorgeous red, white and black.

There are plenty of viceroys in all our eastern and central states. They particularly like open places where there are nectar-bearing flowers of different kinds. Although they look very much like monarchs, you can tell the two apart by the more rapid strokes of a viceroy's wings.

In the forested parts of Canada and the northern United States, you often see a quite different kind of brush-footer. This is the gorgeous red, white and black admiral butterfly. It is also called the banded purple, because of a great white stripe across both sides of its wings. And farther south there is its very close relative, the red-spotted purple, which has no white bars. Both of these butterflies are famous for their striking beauty.

Most of the butterflies we have been talking about prefer to live in sunny, open places. But these two good-sized purples are creatures of the woods. You often see them flying along a shaded road or forest edge. Many times they have favorite perches where they sit quietly and apparently rest. They also gather in muddy places on the ground as if they enjoyed a friendly party.

Their larvae look and behave much like a viceroy's and feed on the same sorts of leaves. And, like baby viceroy caterpillars, they spend their first winter inside silk-lined leaves without freezing to death.

A Born Fighter

One of the prettiest and scrappiest brush-footers is the little buckeye butterfly. It is about the size of a painted lady. And it is just as fond of chasing and attacking other butterflies as the painted lady is. A buckeye has been known to pick quarrels even with large grass-hoppers. But it is much prettier than any painted lady ever dreamed of being.

The general color of this little chap is warm, soft brown. On the upperside of the forewings there are short red bars and a large black eyespot. There are two eyespots on each of the rear wings. The upper one of these is a whopper and has red as well as purple in it. It is so big and staring that it looks almost like the eye of a buck deer. This is where the name buckeye comes from.

Buckeyes are among the fastest-flying of all butter-flies, big or little. Their wings have a quick, nervous sort of beat, and they can change direction in a flash. Besides this, they are so wary that catching one is a real job.

This is one of the species that migrate south in the fall, particularly along our ocean beaches and sand dunes. A good many of them hibernate in sheltered hide-outs for the winter. And in the spring their olive-gray and yellow larvae turn into brown pupae a good deal like those of the pearl crescent.

Buckeyes have many strange ways that no one fully understands. For instance, those which emerge as adults in the spring are darker than the summer ones. Those with birthdays in the summer are very active and do most of the migrating. On the other hand, spring and early autumn adults are likely to be slow-moving and do not migrate. But in spite of these differences, buck-eyes are found all the way from Canada to tropical America.

My own top favorite in the whole vast butterfly group is the brush-footed mourning cloak. It was given this odd name because of the black and white "mourning" markings on the undersides of its wings. You can find it all over North America, Europe, northern Asia and Africa.

On our side of the Atlantic, mourning cloaks are the first butterflies that you see in the spring. They have spent the winter hibernating in sheltered places such as tree holes, old stumps and hollow logs, sheds and even empty barrels. As soon as the weather starts to warm up, they come out of their hiding places and fly around. You often find them perched on sunny, sheltered stumps and tree trunks while patches of snow are still on the ground. At such times they slowly spread and then close their wings as though they thoroughly enjoy stretching and getting warm again.

Mourning cloaks are among the handsomest and best

With its wings spread, the mourning cloak butterfly is gay and colorful. When it alights, you see only the dull undersides.

camouflaged butterflies in the world. The upper sides of their wings are deep chocolate brown with edgings of creamy yellow. Just inside these edges there are black bands dotted with blue spots. The outer margins are so irregular that they look as if they had been torn.

When a mourning cloak alights, it usually lifts its wings and holds them together above its back. Then you can see their undersides, which are quite dull in color and marked with irregular lines. The butterfly is now nearly invisible because it looks so much like its bark or dead-leaf background. It is a perfect example of protective coloration.

A mourning cloak larva is black with little white dots and some red ones. Its five rear pairs of legs are brick red. And all along the back there are stiff spines with many tiny prongs.

This queer-looking caterpillar feeds on many kinds of leaves. Willows, poplars and elms are a few of its favorites. And when the right time comes, it turns into a weird, brown chrysalis with points sticking out along one side.

Bits of Flying Blue and Gray

Soon after the first mourning cloaks have come out of hiding to greet the spring, another much smaller butterfly appears. It is the spring azure, and it does not have brush feet. Its wings spread to only about an inch. As you see it fluttering slowly here and there, it seems even smaller than this, for all four wings are thin and delicate. Their upper sides are a lovely soft blue. Underneath they are very pale except for many scattered dark spots.

These dainty spring insects came from scraps of brownish chrysalises that spent the winter strapped to the undersides of slender twigs. The larvae which fastened them there were rose-tinted white, with decorations of short white hair. And the leaves these little beauties ate were almost anything from clover up to willows.

The true spring azure is at home throughout the eastern part of North America from Canada to Georgia. Slightly different varieties of it are found from the Atlantic to the Pacific and down into Central America. So we might say that the species ranges over all North America except the Arctic.

Bushy areas and rather open, leafy woods are the best places to see it. Sometimes it flies quite high among the branches, especially those of dogwoods. And, like many other butterflies, it often visits damp and even muddy patches of ground.

Another common, very small species that appears later in the season has been given the peculiar name of gray hairstreak. The "gray" part is easy to understand, for that is the principal color of the undersides of its otherwise dark brown wings. But why "hairstreak"?

One reason for this second half of the name is the

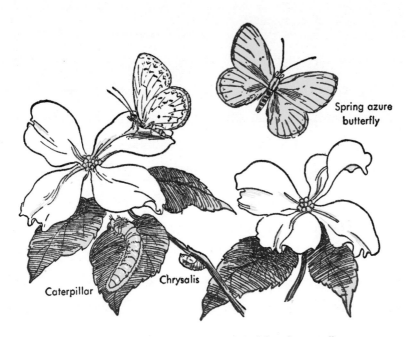

Spring azure
butterfly

Caterpillar

Chrysalis

The spring azure is a tiny soft blue butterfly.

two very slender, almost hairlike tails on each hind wing. There are also very fine, wavy lines crossing the undersides of the wings as if they were hairs. But as you watch one of the little speedsters in the air, you may think that he won his name because he goes so fast. He really does fly like a streak!

Right next to where the two tails join the rear wings there is a single blue and red spot on the upper side. And on the underside there are two such spots. These are the only brilliant colors on the entire butterfly. But they are wonderfully beautiful in their quiet gray setting.

This active, miniature butterfly is plentiful all the way from southern Canada to the Gulf of Mexico and into Central America. It feeds on many different kinds of flowers that grow in meadows and along open roadsides. Some of the favorite foods of its bare-skinned, brown larvae are the leaves of hop vines, garden beans, hawthorns and several kinds of wildflowers.

One of the other butterflies found over almost all of North America is the common sulphur. It is about twice the size of a spring azure. As you might expect from its name, its wings are pale sulphur yellow with black borders at their ends. There are also a few black, red and silver spots.

The sulphurs are often called yellow mud-puddle butterflies because you frequently see swarms of them on wet country roads. A clover or an alfalfa field is another popular gathering place. There, on a warm, sunny day, the air looks as if it were filled with flickering yellow snowflakes. You almost never see a sulphur in a shaded place.

You could search for a long time without finding a

smoother, neater looking caterpillar than the common sulphur. It is grass green with a narrow, yellowish stripe along each side and a dark green one down the middle of the back. There are usually three broods of them during the season, and the last ones turn into attractive green chrysalises which live through the winter.

Champion Traveler

No butterfly could look more unlike a sulphur than the monarch does. This showy, much bigger fellow is red-brown marked with black and white. Its wings spread to about four inches, and the whole effect catches your attention the moment you see it.

But the monarch's size and beauty are not nearly so remarkable as some of the things it does. It can fly as fast as twenty-five miles an hour and has often been seen far out at sea. In some unexplained way it has crossed both the Pacific and Atlantic Oceans and made itself very much at home in foreign lands.

The eggs of this bold wanderer are always laid on a leaf of some kind of milkweed. When the pale green baby caterpillars bite their way out into the open air, they are only about an eighth of an inch long. But they immediately start eating the leaves and growing rapidly.

In a short time they are too big for their first skins and have to change into larger ones. This molt changes their appearance completely. From end to end they are now covered with bright bands or rings of yellow, black and white. From their backs, just behind the head, two black, whiplike "horns" curve forward and upward. And at the tail end there are two smaller ones.

Of course, all this bright coloring makes the caterpillars very easy to see. You would think that any bird passing by would spot one immediately and have a nice juicy meal right then and there. But no bird would ever try such a thing more than once. And here is why:

Milkweed leaves and the milky sap inside them have a very bad taste. Sometimes they can even be poisonous. So, because this caterpillar eats only milkweed, he also tastes terribly bitter. For this reason many birds have learned to leave him absolutely alone. If any other creature starts to get fresh with a monarch larva, those long front "horns" start thrashing around wildly and may drive it away.

In a couple of weeks the monarch-to-be is fully

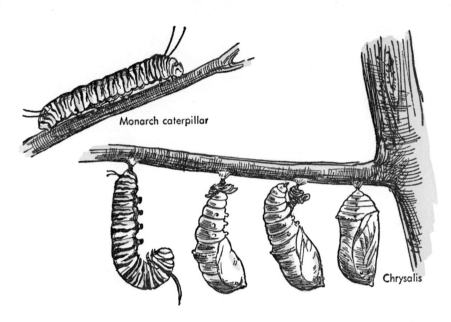

Monarch caterpillar

Chrysalis

Here you see how the monarch caterpillar develops its chrysalis.

grown and nearly two inches long. The time has come for it to turn into one of the most beautiful of all butterfly chrysalises. Its pupal case is a wonderful green decorated with small spots that look like pure gold. Through it, after a day or so, you can see the developing butterfly's folded wings, legs, proboscis and antennae. A little later, the strong colors of these parts will also appear. And in from two to a dozen days, depending largely on how warm the weather is, the perfect adult will emerge. Then it works the wrinkles out of its wings and flies away.

The body of a mature monarch butterfly is just as bitter-tasting as its caterpillar was. The result is that this sturdy flier has little to fear from hungry birds or other natural enemies. It seems to know this instinctively, and so it is a good deal tamer than other butterflies. Sometimes a monarch will perch quietly on a flower and almost let you catch it with your hands. And often it will "play dead" for a minute or two.

Monarchs are strong but dignified in their manner of flying. Usually they give a few flaps and then sail along on motionless wings for quite a distance. In this way they actually travel from Canada to Mexico in their famous autumn migration. At such times they often fly several hundred feet above the ground.

Very few if any monarchs remain in the North during the winter. If they tried to, even as eggs or chrysalises, they would be killed by the cold. Yet every spring they reappear, lay new eggs, and soon their numbers rapidly increase.

People have known for a long time that this reappearance must be the result of a northward migration in the spring. But for a long time no one knew just how this return flight worked. It did not seem possible for any monarch to live long enough to fly to Texas or Mexico in September and back to New England in May. Scientists have now solved the puzzle, which is really a rather simple one:

There are several broods, or generations, of monarchs every year. The adults which make the fall migration came out of their northern pupal stage in late summer or early autumn. Probably they belonged to the last brood. So they were young and strong when they started their southward journey.

Monarch butterflies often travel as far as from Canada to Mexico.

All winter these travelers loaf around in the warm climate of the South. Spring begins early down there. And when it comes, those monarchs which are still alive start to follow the warming weather northward. They are old now, as butterflies go, so they travel slowly. After flying for a while some of them stop and lay eggs. Others do the same thing a little farther north.

Probably none of them ever gets back to the northern states where it grew up. But these old, tired migrants have left millions of eggs along the way. The eggs soon produce fresh caterpillars, these turn into pupae, and then strong young butterflies emerge. These new monarchs, flying northward themselves, finish the long journey which their parents were unable to complete. There they lay eggs of their own, and so last year's story starts all over again.

During the northward migration each monarch travels more or less by itself. In the fall, though, the southbound migrants often gather by thousands to spend the night in trees and bushes. The strangest part of this flocking habit is that the butterflies use the same localities, and often the very same sleeping trees, year after year.

It is not at all unusual for monarchs to attack other kinds of butterflies. They nearly always win these battles, too. One observer reports having seen a monarch go for a hummingbird as though he wanted to beat the life out of it.

The Queer Story of Skippers

Besides the true butterflies, there is another large group of Lepidoptera whose members look as though they were part butterfly and part moth. These odd insects are found all over the world. Their bodies are thicker and their front wings shorter and more pointed than those of regular butterflies. They fly fast and with so many jerky darts that they are called skippers. In general they are stronger and tougher than true butterflies.

Most of these "in-between" insects have more or less the same appearance and general habits. If you take a good look at just one kind you will have a pretty good idea of what the others are like. So here, as a sort of sample, is the species known as the silver-spotted skipper.

The silver-spotted is common along roadsides and in fields and flower gardens from southern Canada to South

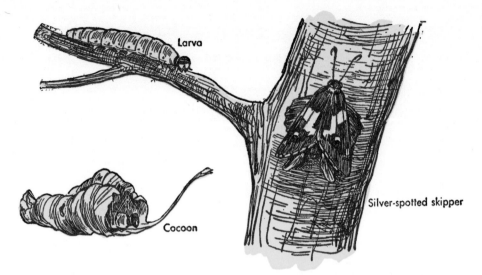

Larva

Cocoon

Silver-spotted skipper

The skipper looks as though it is part butterfly and part moth.

America. The only regions where you may not see it are Texas and the lower part of Florida. It is dark brown with yellowish markings across its front wings. On the underside of each hind wing there is a clearly marked white or "silver" spot.

Its wings spread a little less than two inches. When the insect is resting, the front wings are often held together above the back and the rear ones straight out at the sides. All four wings look as stiff as if they were locked in position. Most other skippers rest in the same peculiar fashion.

It is not surprising that this strong, speedy butterfly

picks many fights with other kinds. Such battles often take place when the skipper is feeding on a flower and does not want anybody else to share the meal. Almost any kind of blossom is likely to attract a silver-spotted.

This skipper's larva gives you a new idea of what a caterpillar can look like. It is smooth and yellow, and its body is much thinner at the ends than in the middle. Its brownish red head has a couple of orange spots that look like eyes. And it lives in a nest made from the leaves of the plant on which it feeds.

When pupation time approaches, this funny little caterpillar crawls down its feeding tree to the ground. There it chooses a hidden leaf, draws the edges around itself like a shawl, and spins a thin cocoon inside. In this flimsy shelter it turns into a pupa which hibernates all winter and until spring is well on its way.

Warm-Country Beauties

In South Carolina, Florida and other states where the winters are really warm you find a very different-looking butterfly. Its name is just plain zebra because of the remarkable way its wings are striped. It is not related in any way to the zebra swallowtail.

This zebra butterfly belongs to a tropical tribe of true butterflies called Heliconians. Its long, rather narrow wings measure about four inches across. And their color is a wonderful combination of pure black crossed with long yellow stripes. Many of its cousins, that live still farther south, are even more brilliant.

Zebras are insects of the deep woods. There, among the shadows, they fly slowly and with very short wing beats. They seem like rather weak, gentle creatures, especially when night comes and they gather to sleep in flocks in favorite trees and bushes.

Their larvae feed on the leaves of passionflowers, which are poisonous to most other animals. This gives them a bitter taste, just as milkweed leaves make the monarch caterpillars bitter. And, like the monarchs, zebra butterflies inherit this flavor and so are protected from birds. Maybe this is one reason for their easy-going flight.

The zebra is only one of many amazingly colorful butterflies that live in the tropical parts of the New World. From Mexico south through Central America and on to the great jungles of South America, you can find hundreds of species too brilliant to believe until

Zebra butterflies

At night zebra butterflies gather in flocks in trees.

you have actually seen them. Blue, flaming red, gold, green, purple, orange and jet black—these are just a few of their colors.

Callitheas are among the most sparkling of these tropical butterflies. The upper sides of their wings glitter with sapphire and turquoise colors. And these dazzling hues change and change again according to the direction of the light and the angle from which you see them.

It is a peculiar fact that these changing colors are not built into the wings. Instead, they are caused by the way the light is reflected from countless tiny, colorless structures located in the wing scales. These little particles "break up" the different colors which, when combined, form what we call daylight. It's like this:

Daylight is a combination of several colors. Under the right conditions these are separated and reflected by drops of water. This is what happens in a rainbow. A diamond will break up the colors in white light in the same way. You have probably seen a diamond flash red, blue, green or some other color when you hold it in different positions. Well, the special wing structures of the tropical butterflies can do the same thing.

The largest of these gleaming butterflies in the American tropics are called morphos. Some species of them spread as much as seven inches across. Most kinds are a gorgeous blue or blue and black. Others are orange, green and black, lavender, or glistening white. The flashes from their marvelous wings can be seen a quarter of a mile away. They seem like brilliant reflections from colored mirrors. Plane passengers looking down as they fly over the jungle sometimes see these glittering lights in the treetops far below them.

A companion and I found many of these great morphos when we were on a long collecting expedition in South America. They spent most of their time high up among the tall jungle trees. But on clear mornings they would come quite close to the ground in open spots where there was some sunlight.

The most popular of these sunny visiting places was along a one-track railroad that cut a narrow pathway through the thick jungle near one of our camps. Only two short trains a week used the rusty rails, so the butterflies did not have much to frighten them while they were there.

Morpho after morpho would sail along this railroad trail with only an occasional flap of its broad, shining wings. They looked easy to catch, but we quickly learned that they were experts at escaping. Perhaps they saw us coming, or knew in some other way that we might be dangerous. Time after time they would vanish into the jungle long before we were close enough to use our butterfly nets. When we did manage to make a sweep at one, it usually got away by dodging with surprising speed.

In ten days we were able to capture only three. One of these, believe it or not, sat quietly in the grass beside our thatched lean-to camp until I clapped my hat over it.

The larva of a morpho may be as much as four inches long. Some kinds are purple with red and black tufts on their backs. One has a thick fringe of blond hair along each side. Yes, they are almost as colorful as their parents.

Among the smaller butterflies that we often saw near the ground in the jungle depths were the Haeteras. Their wings spread as much as three inches, and you can see through them almost as easily as if they were made of glass. Dr. C. William Beebe, the famous naturalist, called them "ghost butterflies." That was because their wings are almost colorless and look ghostly as they fly through the gloomy jungle shadows. One species which he found in British Guiana was completely without color except for three little spots of blue near the edge of each hind wing.

I remember especially one of these ghostlike insects

Ghost butterfly

You can see through the wings of a ghost butterfly as easily as if they were made of plastic.

that flitted across a narrow, misty trail a few feet ahead of me. Apparently it lighted on a broad, dull green leaf. Yet when I walked slowly forward for a better look, no butterfly was to be seen. Finally, from very close range, I made out the insect's body and the faint outline of its spread wings. The green color of that big leaf showing through the wings made the Haetera practically invisible. You could not imagine a more perfect camouflage system than the one that little "ghost" carried in its own four transparent wings.

Moth and Butterfly Enemies

There are so many trillions of moths and butterflies in the tropics and other parts of the world, and they lay such a terrific number of eggs every year, that you may wonder why they have not taken possession of the entire earth. Perhaps they would have done so long ago if they had been left to themselves. But there are huge armies of other creatures which prey on them and so prevent their becoming too numerous.

Other kinds of insects are the worst enemies that moths and butterflies have. Among the most important of these are various members of the Wasp Order, such as the *ichneumons, chalcids* and *brachonids*. Besides these there are *tachnid* flies, some of which look a good deal like ordinary houseflies. Many of these flying enemies are very small, and some others have wingspreads of two inches or more. All those I have mentioned are called *parasites* because they must make victims of other insects in order to keep their own families going.

These parasitic insects lay their eggs on or in many kinds of moth and butterfly larvae. When the eggs hatch, the baby larvae chew their way into their unlucky "host" until he is nearly dead. By that time they are old enough to pupate and turn into flying creatures like their parents. The host caterpillar, though, has been so weakened by their feeding that it may not have enough strength to pupate at all. Even if it does manage to start

Millions of moths and butterflies are devoured by birds.

pupation, it cannot finish the job. Most of its insides have been eaten away, and so it dies without having a chance to turn into an adult flier.

This is the way most parasites work. But a few kinds are so extremely small that they lay their own eggs inside the tiny eggs of both moths and butterflies before the caterpillars hatch out. Then the larvae either do not hatch at all, or die soon after they emerge.

Birds, too, play an important part in controlling the moth and butterfly population. For example, the night-feeding whip-poor-wills eat great numbers of adult moths, particularly the large species. Cuckoos are fond of tent caterpillar meals. Different kinds of flycatchers and other insect-eating birds gobble millions of butterflies and moths. Some of them swallow even greater numbers of insect eggs and larvae. And finally, huge quantities of these insects, in one stage or another, fall victims to hungry frogs, toads, lizards, turtles, fish, dragonflies, spiders, robber flies, and even monkeys and some other small mammals.

Altogether, the moth or butterfly that lives long enough to grow up is a rather lucky insect!

Of course, all moths and butterflies have ways of escaping their enemies. Some get away by fast flying or expert dodging. Others are protectively colored, produce unpleasant smells, or fight back when attacked. Suddenly changing the color effect by hiding bright rear wings under dull front ones is another escape trick. And, as you remember, certain species avoid being caught by imitating the appearance of some other bad-tasting kind such as the monarch. These are probably the most important ways they have of saving their own lives.

How to Study Moths and Butterflies

Starting the Search

Watching moths and butterflies as they live their amazing lives can be a great deal of fun. It is easy, too, for there are so many of them that you are sure to find some almost anywhere you go. Even fair-sized city parks have a surprising variety of them. Several times I have seen monarchs and sulphurs flying down Fifth Avenue, in New York!

When you go out to look for these marvelous insects, remember that many kinds like special sorts of places.

Some prefer woods, others choose dry, brushy fields or flower gardens. Many other kinds are found in swamps, damp meadows, alfalfa fields, or perhaps seacoast dunes and marshes. In general, any place where there are plenty of flowers is popular among butterflies and the smaller moths. The best seasons for seeing them are spring, summer and early fall.

Another helpful idea is to look for the kinds of food plants which different species prefer. For example, the best place to find monarchs—except when they are migrating—is a patch of milkweed. Spicebush swallowtails, as you know, often hang around spicebushes.

When you are looking for caterpillars, it is particularly important to find the plants on which they feed. Experts on moth and butterfly life can go into a perfectly strange neighborhood and quickly tell what species can probably be found there. They do this by noticing the kinds of food plants and the places where they grow.

Most caterpillars are hard to see because they move very slowly and are protectively colored. One way to spot them is to watch for leaves which have been eaten and carefully examine them as well as others near by.

Such leaves may be on a wild or garden plant, a bush, tree or vine, depending on what species is feeding on them. The damage usually shows along the edges, where small pieces have been bitten out. Sometimes there are holes clear through the middle part of the leaf. And now and then you will find a leaf that has been completely eaten except for its central vein or "rib."

Another sign to watch for is a leaf, or maybe several leaves, whose edges have been rolled or pulled together. This may be a nest that some caterpillar has made with the help of a little silk. If you pull it apart, you may find the builder hiding inside.

Sometimes you can locate a large caterpillar, like a polyphemus or luna, by seeing its droppings or "frass" on the ground. Usually the caterpillar is directly above these droppings. It may be feeding on tree leaves that grow higher than your head. Then, of course, you will have to look upward. This method of discovery is particularly successful if the ground under the feeding plant is bare of leaves and other trash. The droppings show very clearly in such places.

Adult moths are harder to find than butterflies because most of them stay in hiding until nightfall. But there are several ways in which you can see surprising numbers of them.

On almost any late spring or summer evening around nine o'clock many of these night-fliers will gather outside lighted windows. You can get a fairly good view of them from inside the house. But it is much better to go outside and stand quietly a few feet from the side of the window. Most species are quite tame and will pay little attention to you. A flashlight will often help you get a better view of one that has perched on the frame of the window where the light from inside does not reach it.

A still better plan is to take up your position near a powerful outdoor electric light of some sort. A floodlight that is used to light up your doorway, entrance gate or parking space often attracts so many moths of different kinds that the air is filled with them swooping and darting in all directions. Arc lights at street corners in small towns and villages are good gathering places, too, particularly late at night. The trouble with them is that most of these lights are too high for you to get really good views of the insects that come to them. But it is exciting to watch the moths appearing, disappearing and returning again as if by magic.

On a spring evening a floodlight will attract swarms of moths.

It is worth remembering that many good-sized species are drawn from far away by the smell of rotted fruit, fermenting fruit juice, manure and other queer things. Moths like to feed on them, and so do many butterflies. Insect authorities discovered this habit many years ago and figured out a way to make it useful to them. It is an idea that works just as well today, too. And here it is:

First, get a pail and dump two pounds of sugar into it. Then pour in half a bottle of beer. Stir the mixture until all the sugar is dissolved. It will make a smelly, sticky, sweetish sort of mess that no human being would even taste. But insects are crazy about it.

In the late evening, while there is still light enough for you to see what you are doing, take an old brush and smear gobs of this stuff on the trunks of several trees. An hour or two later, go back to look at these spots with a flashlight. There is a good chance that you will see some splendid moths having a grand meal.

It is a good idea for you to make the rounds of these "bait trees" several times at intervals of a half-hour or so. In this way you are likely to see moths which had not arrived when you made your earlier trips.

Instead of the beer and sugar mixture you can use grape juice, molasses and a cake of yeast. This works best after it has stood in an open jar for several days. By that time it will have started to ferment and will taste wonderful to a moth.

Mixtures like these often attract butterflies during the day, too. So will rotted apples and other fruits. You might even try spoiled fruit juice. And, surprisingly, one of the best butterfly baits is the body of a snake that has been dead long enough to smell bad. Baits are especially useful in the case of species that ordinarily spend most of their time in the treetops. These high-fliers will often come right to the ground to see what all the smell is about.

Perhaps neither moths nor butterflies will find a baited tree for a while. But once they do, more and more of them will come there to feed. So it is worth while to add some fresh bait every day for a week or more.

During the summer you can be sure of finding several species of interesting butterflies feeding on the blossoms of various garden plants. One of the best of these is a good-sized flowering shrub which many people plant on their lawns. Its correct name is buddleia. But it is often called butterfly bush because its pink, red or purple flower spikes are so attractive to these insects. Some other garden plants whose flowers are favorite butterfly feeding places are lilies, petunias, honeysuckle, beauty bush, mock orange (especially for swallowtails), weigela and meadow rue.

Front-Row Seats for the Show

All through this book you have been reading about the interesting habits and lives of moths and butterflies.

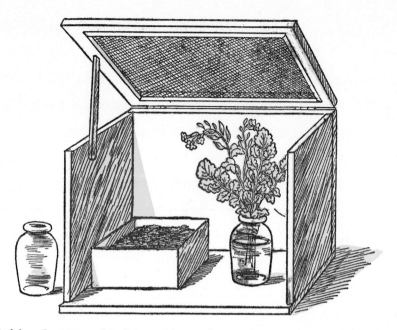

Add a front to this box and you have a fine place to observe moths and butterflies in their strange life cycle.

Would you like to watch their strange doings only a foot or two from your own eyes? Well, you can! It is easy and a lot of fun, too. So here is your plan, beginning with the next fair-sized caterpillar you find chewing away on the leaf of a plant.

First of all, get yourself a wooden box or heavy cardboard carton about a foot and a half square and high. Make a close-fitting cover for it out of four strips of wood on which you have tacked metal window-screen netting or ordinary mosquito netting.

Inside the large box you should have a smaller one

filled with ordinary earth. This will be useful for caterpillars that pupate underground. You will also need two
fairly wide-topped bottles filled with water. Clean pickle
bottles will do very well.

This is the home in which your caterpillar is to live
while you watch it eat, grow, molt and finally pupate.
If everything goes well, you may get a perfect view of
an adult butterfly coming out of the pupal casing in
which it was formed. There is no better way of seeing
for yourself exactly what all these stages in the insect's
life really look like.

Now for the best way to catch a caterpillar and bring
it back alive! For this you should have a sharp knife, one
of the bottles of water, and a little cardboard box with
small holes punched in its cover for ventilation.

Let us suppose that your caterpillar is feeding on a
leafy twig of a tree or shrub. Or maybe it is busy eating
the leaves of some garden flower.

In either case, quietly cut off the stem several inches
below the larva. Be especially careful not to move the
branch suddenly or even jiggle it. This might frighten
the caterpillar and cause it to lose its grip. If it does
happen to fall, try to get it to crawl into your cardboard

box. Sometimes a little gentle poking with a soft grass or weed stem will send it where you want it to go. Or you may have to roll, shove or lift it into the box with your fingers or the box cover.

Next, put the butt-end of the leafy branch in your water bottle to keep it from wilting. If the caterpillar is still on it, try to carry him home without his falling off. In case he takes a tumble, just shut him in the box where he can't get away.

When you get back to the house, put the bottle and the branch in the screened box. Stuff a piece of rag into the mouth of the bottle to hold the branch steady and prevent the caterpillar's falling in accidentally and getting drowned. If the little fellow is still clinging to the leaves, he will start eating again when things quiet down. But in case he is in your cardboard box, you will have to get him back among the leaves the best way you can.

It is very important, of course, to keep the caterpillar well supplied with fresh leaves of the same kind that he was eating when you found him. This is where the second water bottle comes in handy. All you need to do is to put a fresh branch in it and place the two bottles side by side so that their leaves touch. Then the caterpillar can crawl over to its new dinner table whenever it wants to. When this has happened, refill bottle Number One with fresh food to which your caterpillar can return as soon as he finishes with the contents of bottle Number Two. Always remember that moth and butterfly larvae do not like wilted meals.

A screened box like this is called a "breeding cage." It should be kept in an airy place where it will get some sun but be protected from rain. A roofed porch is a good location for it. Or you might put it near a window in your room. Make sure that the lid is tightly closed except when you are right there to catch your friend in case he should crawl out.

When the larva quits eating and starts to wander around, you can be quite sure that it is getting ready to pupate. This is the time for you to look in frequently so as to see what is really happening.

If you have one of the kinds that turn into hanging pupae, like many of the butterflies described in this book, you can watch the whole process from beginning to end. You may even see the pupa change color as the new butterfly begins to take form inside the casing. And, finally, there will be those astonishing minutes when the adult insect struggles out into the open air and you can watch its crumpled wings pumping, straightening out, and actually growing larger.

Should your caterpillar be a kind that pupates underground, you can watch it burrowing into the box of soil. The pupa of such a species almost always spends the winter in the earth. This means that it is perfectly natural for it to become very cold in its hiding place. So, instead of keeping the soil box in the house during the cold weather, put it outside.

If the caterpillar you have been keeping in the breeding cage belongs to a moth instead of a butterfly, the story will be somewhat different, of course. Those that spin cocoons inside the leaves they feed on may do this right there in the cage. Or if yours is a species that chooses some sheltered surface, as woolly bears and tent caterpillars do, it may spin its cocoon on the side of the box. It is hard to be sure about such things as these until they actually happen.

While you are out collecting caterpillars, you will often find freshly laid eggs of moths and butterflies on the leaves of plants. By cutting off those leafy branches and keeping them in water inside the breeding cage, you will have a chance to watch the young caterpillars as they hatch. Not many people have seen that, but it is really worth watching!

And here is another suggestion. Cut off and bring home any twig on which a butterfly pupa is already hanging. Probably the adult will come struggling out of it in a few days or maybe a week or so. Then you can find out what kind it is.

A breeding cage like the one you have made is also a first-class place in which to keep moth cocoons.

As you know, most kinds of moth larvae spin their cocoons above the ground. In a great many cases these cocoons are fastened to the twigs or stems of the plants on which the caterpillars fed while they were growing up.

Your particular caterpillar may do this inside the cage where you can watch how he manages it. It is a good idea to provide him with several small extra branches so that he will have a better chance to find a spot that is exactly right. These branches had better be kept in water, in case the larva is one of the kinds that pupate inside leaves.

Then, when the cocoon is finished, place the cage

outdoors instead of keeping it warm in the house. It should stay outside until the adult emerges. If you kept it in a warm place the pupa might die. Even if it lived, the moth would probably come out so early in the spring that there would be no good, safe place on which it could lay its eggs.

Fun in the Fall

There is another way to make a breeding cage a very worthwhile place. I built my first one just for moth cocoons. That was in late autumn many years ago. During the next summer I fed caterpillars and raised pupae in it, too. So it really was kept busy all through the year.

Collecting "wild" cocoons in the fields and woods around home is even more fun than caterpillar hunting. You begin in the autumn, after the leaves have fallen. At this time the cocoons are easier to spot as they hang from tree twigs, cling to bits of bark, or lie on the surface of the ground. You can collect them all winter, too, and even in early spring before the adults start emerging. And there will be no need for you to equip the breeding cage with water bottles and fresh leaves.

Most of the moth larvae spin their cocoons on the

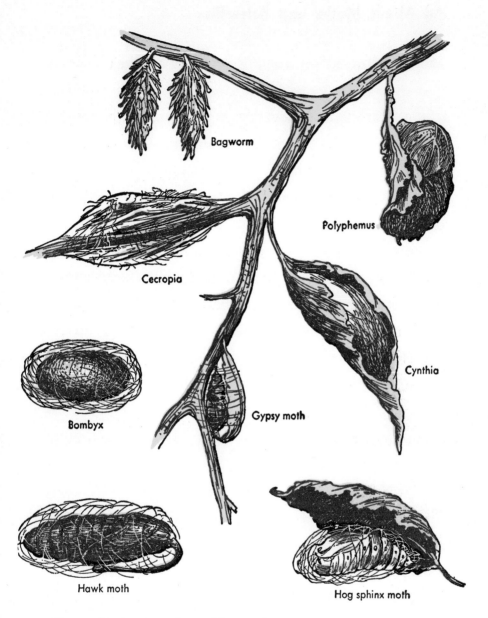

Bagworm

Polyphemus

Cecropia

Cynthia

Bombyx

Gypsy moth

Hawk moth

Hog sphinx moth

Different kinds of moths and butterflies create a strange variety
of cocoons as shown above.

plants whose leaves they eat. So, whenever you see something that looks like a dead leaf still hanging on after all the others have fallen, examine it closely. If there are any signs of silk fastening it to the twig, it is almost certainly a cocoon.

Some of the best plants for cocoons are small wild cherries, spicebush, sweet gum and sassafras. All these are favorites of the promethea moth. Cecropia cocoons are usually in bayberry or other low bushes, but you may find them almost anywhere. Instead of dangling from twigs, they are fastened tightly to fairly upright stems.

Various other large cocoons, such as those of the polyphemus and io species, generally lie right on the ground. The best places to hunt for them are under the feeding trees and bushes. Sometimes they are very hard to see, for they may be almost buried by fallen leaves. So go slowly, watch carefully, and try not to step on any.

While you are poking around among the dead leaves, you may also uncover a sphinx moth cocoon. Some species of this long-tongued tribe spend the winter as pupae deep in the ground. But others spin loose, sloppy-looking cocoons hidden under dead leaves. Any one of them will prove a real treasure. So handle it carefully and follow the directions which I will give you later for taking care of all on-the-ground cocoons.

When you discover one of the many fair-sized cocoons, the first thing to do is to find out if it is "alive." If it looks badly weather-beaten, and has a sort of worn opening at one end, it is probably old and empty. But if it seems fresh, cut off the twig close to where the cocoon is fastened to it. Then test the weight of the cocoon in the palm of your hand. A "live" one is light, but not nearly so light as a "dead" one. Another test is to shake it gently close to your ear. If you can hear a soft clunking inside it, you can be quite sure that this sound is made by a stout, healthy pupa being bounced around a bit.

A little practice in finding large cocoons like these will make it easier for you to spot many kinds of smaller ones. Watch especially for the strange little hanging houses of the bagworms, about which I have already told you. It often pays, too, to look under loose pieces of tree bark, flat stones, and other kinds of protected places. Some of these winter hide-outs will contain only spider egg masses, which look like little white balls. But there will also be moth cocoons of various kinds and shapes. And you are almost sure to find brown or blackish butterfly chrysalises. These you can take home and place under pieces of bark in the breeding cage so as to see what comes out of them in the spring.

When you return home with your cocoons, they should be placed in the cage at once. Those which are attached to twigs can be pinned firmly to different places on the top or sides of the cage where they will hang in a natural position. Others which were found loose on the ground should be laid on damp moss on the cage floor and covered with a few dead leaves. You had better water these leaves a little every few weeks so as to be sure that the cocoons do not dry out too much.

The best way to keep any kinds that are attached to stones or bark is to prop them up against the sides of the box. It is important for all kinds to be in the same general position in which you found them.

Of course, the breeding cage must be kept in a cold but protected place outdoors after the cocoons have been placed in it. If you were to put it in any spot that is artificially heated, the pupae might die or at least be badly weakened. So do not bring the cage into the house until spring.

Here is another tip: keep a wad of damp cloth somewhere in the cage as long as the cocoons are in it. This will prevent the air from becoming so dry that the pupae might be harmed. Nature always provides air dampness by rain, snow, or evaporation from the ground or living plants. But you can get the same results more easily in a breeding cage by using damp cloth. This will keep on doing its job even when it is frozen.

Exciting Days

When will the adult moths start coming out of their cocoons? This depends a good deal on what kinds they are. In general, the time for emerging is from the opening of the first garden daffodils until early summer. Here are the reasons for such a long season:

A moth comes out of its cocoon just in time to mate, lay its eggs, and have those eggs hatch when there is plenty of fresh food for the baby caterpillars to eat. If the moth started laying too soon, the larvae would starve because the leaves would not be large enough to feed on. And if the parent started laying too late, the youngsters would be behind their proper schedule. That would be really serious because it would upset the species' whole life cycle.

Because of all this, the moths that emerge first are those whose caterpillars feed on early-starting plants. Next come those that depend on plants which come into good leaf in mid-spring—when the apple blossoms are about over, let us say. And the latest of all are the big fellows such as lunas and cecropias whose eggs are not laid until the end of spring or the beginning of summer. What it all adds up to is that the time for leaving the cocoon lasts for almost six weeks.

It does not take moths long to get out of their cocoons, once they begin. Often the whole operation lasts only a few minutes. Clear, pleasant and fairly warm weather usually starts them going, because such conditions are favorable for straightening wings, drying off, and finally flying away. So take a look at your breeding cage as often as you can during the spring and early summer. In this way you will see most of the show, if not all of it.

When the moth is ready to fly, the best thing to do is to open the top of the cage and let it go. It will be all

It takes only a few minutes for a moth to come out of its cocoon.

right, though, to keep it for a few hours if you want to study it. And if it happens to be one of the larger species, here is an experiment you really ought to try:

Keep the moth in the cage until after dark. Then set the cage somewhere outdoors, or just inside an open window, with the top closed and the moth inside it. After an hour or so, take a look with the help of a flashlight. Very likely you will see another moth of the same kind (or maybe several of them) fluttering around outside the cage. Then you can be certain of two things:

First, the one that you saw emerge from its cocoon is a female. And second, the visitor is a male which has been guided to her by those marvelous antennae on his head. He may have come from a hundred yards away—or a mile or two! But he found the way just as surely as if she were a magnet and he a little piece of steel attracted by it.

You see a breeding cage for moths and butterflies can be a lot of fun. You can learn strange things from it and see wonderful sights inside its walls. And besides all this, it will help to unlock the door to that marvelous land of Nature that begins right in your own backyard and stretches away to the farthest corners of the world.

Index

Index

Index